PRIVATE EYE

Dr Hammond's
Covid Casebook

D1514359

The collected pandemic columns of
Private Eye's medical correspondent 'MD'

As *Private Eye*'s medical correspondent 'MD', Dr Phil Hammond has written a fortnightly column for the magazine since 1992, when he broke the story of the Bristol heart scandal, later giving evidence to the public inquiry. Having qualified as a doctor in 1987 and as a GP in 1991, he worked part-time in general practice and sexual health for 20 years, and was a lecturer in medical communication at the universities of Birmingham and Bristol. For the last decade, he has worked in an NHS team for young people with severe fatigue, including post-viral fatigue. In 2011, he was shortlisted for the Martha Gellhorn Prize for Journalism, with Andrew Bousfield, for Shooting the Messenger, a *Private Eye* special report on the shocking treatment of NHS whistleblowers.

Private Eye Productions Limited
6 Carlisle Street, London, W1D 3BN

www.private-eye.co.uk

First Published in Great Britain by Private Eye Productions Limited 2021
1 3 5 7 9 10 8 6 4 2
Copyright © Pressdram Limited / Dr Phil Hammond 2021

A catalogue record for this book is available from the British Library
PB ISBN 978-1-901784-71-8

Printed and bound in Great Britain by Clays Limited, Suffolk NR35 1ED

A Doctor writes...

THERE are two views on how the UK has handled the SARS-CoV-2 pandemic so far.

One, expressed by prime minister Boris Johnson, is that "We truly did everything we could, and continue to do everything that we can, to minimise loss of life and to minimise suffering." The other is that for a wealthy island nation with world-leading public health expertise, we didn't truly do all we could to minimise loss and suffering, and as a result have endured unprecedented avoidable deaths and harm.

It will be for a public inquiry to decide which view is most accurate and the degree to which the UK was ill-prepared, was confused and contradictory in its strategy and should have acted more quickly from the start. But we already know we didn't take advantage of our island geography, and that those leading us through the pandemic do not seem to have learnt from their mistakes. Even before our exemplary vaccine programme is completed, we continue to import new variants of the virus in large numbers, causing yet more avoidable harm and delaying our return to a more normal life.

Science learns by forming a hypothesis and then trying to prove it wrong; errors are welcomed, accepted and improved upon. But politics struggles to embrace this scientific method. If the pandemic teaches us the need for a more honest and open approach to politics, that will be one improvement.

Over the course of the pandemic I have written 30 fortnightly updates and counting, and have tried to be broad and balanced. I have not always succeeded and am grateful to those readers who have spotted my errors along the way.

Dr Phil Hammond, aka 'MD'

The daily case and death figures quoted at the start of
the following columns are the rolling seven-day
averages at the time *Private Eye* went to press.
(Source: *coronavirus.data.gov.uk*, "Deaths within
28 days of positive test by date reported".)

MD on The best medicine

Private Eye 1518   Press day: 16 March 2020
383 daily cases   **21** daily deaths   **65** UK deaths to date

Testing times

WHY has the UK government stopped population testing of coronavirus?

It plans to protect the most at risk by asking them to self-isolate for up to 14 weeks (at a date to be announced), while allowing the least at risk to become infected in a phased manner that establishes herd immunity and avoids overloading the NHS. This is highly speculative and at odds with the policies of many other countries and the World Health Organization.

As WHO director-general Tedros Adhanom Ghebreyesus puts it: "The idea that countries should shift from containment to mitigation is wrong and dangerous." Many UK scientists are also deeply sceptical of this approach; and the government urgently needs to release the modelling that informs it. Stopping community testing makes any plan less likely to succeed.

How will the government know when to step up "social distancing", whether it has succeeded in flattening the curve or if it has got things badly wrong if it has stopped collecting data? How will NHS and social care staff know when it's safe to return to work after infection, if they don't even know if they've been infected? If you don't measure, you can't manage. And you can't fight a virus if you don't know where it is.

Funeral march

FROM the moment your sperm meets your egg, you join the queue for death. It's nature's way of recycling. You can fall back in the queue by eating your greens or washing your hands, but we all get to the front eventually. Even experts have been known to die.

In 2018-2019, there were 541,589 deaths registered in England and Wales, 50,100 more than expected, due to a mixture of cold weather, prolonged austerity and seasonal respiratory viruses. Pandemics grow exponentially and cases could quickly overwhelm the NHS, social care and funeral services, and cause widespread cancellation of treatment for other conditions like cancer and heart disease.

Estimates of how many extra deaths Covid-19 will cause in the UK range from 50,000 (similar to 2018-19) to 500,000 (a doubling of annual deaths). It all depends how well we manage the risks. The government's policy is to abandon containment and promote herd immunity, with Public Health England now anticipating the crisis could last a year, infect 80 percent of the population and lead to 7.9m people needing hospitalisation. This would likely put the deaths at the upper end of the estimates, and intensive care would have to be strictly rationed.

Hand-washing: a roaring success

THE government's scaling back of community testing has fuelled further uncertainty. But the hand-washing campaign at least has been a roaring success. Early figures suggest it may have delayed the surge of Covid-19, and is likely to have reduced the incidence of seasonal influenza, food poisoning, hepatitis A, threadworm and pubic hair in Caesar salad. Alas, 40 percent of the world's population do not have access to the miracle of soap and water in their homes, and that is where the virus will eventually hit hardest.

For the UK public at large, the risk of a coronavirus death remains low. The predicted range is that out of every 100 random Brits, 99 won't die from Covid-19 this year (worst scenario) to out of every 1,000 people, 999 won't die from Covid-19 (best scenario).

Those at highest risk are in their 80s – not surprisingly since the average life expectancy in the UK is 81.25 years. Those who die may have died from something else in the not too distant future. If MD (58) became seriously ill with Covid-19, I'd join the queue for a ventilator but accept if a 40-year-old jumped ahead of me. That's how rationing in the NHS has always worked. If I make it to 80, I would neither want nor expect to have prolonged intubation on ITU for severe respiratory distress. Overtreatment of the elderly when they are seriously ill often just extends suffering. Before we all demanded to live forever, pneumonia was known as "the old man's friend" (with a dose of morphine on top).

Experts have been predicting another pandemic for decades, but politicians refused to listen, preferring to run the NHS on near 100 per cent bed occupancy, with fewer beds and intensive care facilities than most other countries. Indeed, over the last 30 years, the number of NHS hospital beds has halved. We have not built extra capacity into the system and we will soon find out if we can.

All eyes will now switch to the overall death figures. The Office for National Statistics provides a weekly tally for those with a strong stomach. The week ending 10 January 2020 was the worst of the year so far, with 14,058 deaths. It's fallen every week since to 10,816 in the week ended 28 February. Deaths are actually lower this year than the average for each week over the previous five years. I like to think it's the handwashing.

Bingeing on fear

MANY countries have taken much stricter measures than the UK, based on roughly the same evidence, which shows how uncertain the science is. We will only find out who got it right after the event. In the UK, many older people may say "bollocks" to 14 weeks of lockdown and go about what's left of their once wild and precious life. All adults should already have made an Advanced Care Plan (eg via Compassion in Dying), so doctors know whether they want a shot at recovery or end of life care.

MD works in the world of post-viral fatigue and is expecting an increase in workload down the line. Evidence suggests that if you're fearful and anxious when and after you contract a virus, it makes the symptoms and long-term sequelae worse. And the UK is currently bingeing on fear.

Down the corridor, my anaesthetist colleagues have started their spike in workload. The Chinese and Italian experience is that staff working in intensive care may be at greater risk of serious illness and death. This may be because repeated exposure to high doses of the virus from intubation and other intimate procedures takes its toll. It may be that the best protective equipment wasn't available. And it may also be that the stress and fear of working intolerably long hours with a relentless workload of critically ill infectious patients also damages the immune system and makes you more susceptible. By any projection, we are not well equipped to deal with a surge in demand. ITU staff need the best equipment available. And the right to refuse to treat.

GPs and other community carers are doing home visits to people likely to have Covid-19 without any protective equipment at all, or with cut price garb that looks like they work behind the counter in Greggs. How virus-tight they are remains to be seen, but they are causing much nervous hilarity.

Keep it up

LAUGHTER is the best medicine, unless you have syphilis, in which case it's penicillin. There are no effective drugs yet for Covid-19 and the best ways to boost your immune system are not the nonsense new age supplements doing the rounds (there's a $200 magic yoghurt pill you can shove up your arse) but laughter and sex. The second drug my GP surgery ran out of (after paracetamol) was Viagra. The best position for reduced transmission and improved lung function is the wheelbarrow. Just don't go past your mum's house.

Enjoy your isolation. Look out for others. Try not to fall down the stairs. Don't get caught in a bog-roll scrum (the ideal breeding-ground for viruses). And remember it's the simple pleasures, not the big scares, that give purpose and meaning to life. Coronavirus may yet teach us to behave in a kinder, gentler, less consumptive way.

10-13 March: Cheltenham Festival goes ahead with full crowds. **11 Mar**: Liverpool FC host Atletico Madrid, with 3,000 visiting Spanish fans. **12 Mar**: Government to stop community testing and focus on testing in hospitals and protecting health workers, as it moves from "contain" to "delay". **16 Mar**: PM says "now is the time for everyone to stop non-essential contact and travel", as Imperial College London modellers find critical care capacity in the UK will be overwhelmed and 250,000 people will die unless social distancing is put in place. **17 Mar**: First use of the word "lockdown" in SAGE minutes.

MD on The Great British fudge

Private Eye 1519   **Press day: 30 March**
3,279 daily cases   **414** daily deaths   **2,050 UK** deaths to date

Do or die

WHAT's most striking about Britain's idiosyncratic approach to the coronavirus pandemic is the lack of public support from senior scientists and public health experts outside the government circle.

Most support Boris Johnson's belated attempt at lockdown but worry that the UK is two weeks behind the curve, notably in London. Many believe he wasted nine weeks on "nuanced nudging" when the evidence from China and Italy was clear that tougher methods would be needed. Many remain incredulous at the lack of testing and contact tracing, not just in the community but of NHS staff, who don't know if they have it so err on the side of caution and remain off work.

Johnson has ignored the evidence-based advice of pandemic experts at the World Health Organization and gone it alone. Britain is forging a brave new path in the new era of pandemics. Will we take back control of the virus in 12 weeks, as the PM says, do or die; or lose control of all the other things that kill us?

Bug's life

A VIRUS, according to the late Nobel Prize-winning immunologist Sir Peter Medawar, is "simply a piece of bad news wrapped up in protein". How bad depends on whether you've had it before.

This particular coronavirus is "novel"; our immune systems have never seen its RNA message, so the damage it's causing is significant, particularly for those with bodies weakened by age and disease. The virus exists merely to replicate and is extraordinarily good at it. The saliva of Covid-19 patients can contain half a trillion virus particles per teaspoon. A cough or a sneeze shoots out a mist of millions which hang around in the air long enough for you to take in tens of thousands of virus particles in a single breath, in between your husband's coughing fits. The most successful viruses learn to live in their hosts, rather than kill them. If the host dies, they die. The problem is, humans aren't a natural host for these SARS (severe acute respiratory syndrome) viruses.

How to stop a pandemic

IN the SARS outbreak of 2003, there were no deaths in Britain thanks to brilliant global public health cooperation. Important lessons were widely shared about control of future disease outbreaks in an excellent book, *SARS – How a Global Epidemic Was Stopped* (WHO).

"Transparency," it said, "is the best policy. Some countries did not acknowledge openly the presence of SARS or downplayed its extent. One nation's weak response could endanger the world's public health security. 21st-century science played a relatively small role in controlling SARS; 19th-century techniques continued to prove their value." Developing diagnostic tests was crucial, and then the old methods of relentless testing, contact tracing and isolation stopped it becoming a pandemic.

Another lesson was that "animal husbandry and marketing practices seriously affect human health". The 2003 SARS coronavirus originated in animals. Indeed, 75 percent of emerging infectious diseases come from domestic or wild animals. Bats, birds, pigs, pangolins. Surely we've learned the lessons of 2003?

Bat-shit crazy

A STUDY of the SARS-CoV-2 virus genome published in *Nature* on 17 March has pinned it not on mad scientists wanting to rule the world, but on bats. It probably crossed to humans in the live animal markets of Wuhan – a perfect storm for transmission.

The virus was on the wall in 2003, but unhygienic veterinary, slaughter and husbandry practices, and an illegal global trade in exotic animals for food, have continued unabated. Bats are fortunately a protected species in the UK, even when Waitrose has run out of grouse. Elsewhere, they should only be sold pre-cooked, chlorinated or as part of a ready meal.

No place like home

THE Chinese got off to a slow start with Covid-19, trying to cover up the outbreak in Wuhan. A brave whistleblowing doctor, Li Wenliang, tried to raise concerns but was targeted by the Chinese police for scaremongering and subsequently died, reportedly of Covid-19. Then China delayed reporting the outbreak to the world, until it became so big you could see it from space. Finally, they remembered the chapter in the book on transparency and started sharing their expertise.

The Chinese realised from previous SARS outbreaks that most spread occurs in family groups, and the last thing you want to do is isolate them all in a house together. Random temperature checks, virus testing and contact tracing on a grand and relentless scale is followed by separation from family and transfer to a hospital for the really sick, or to a massive sanatorium full of other Covid-19 patients for the rest. It's the only way to break the chain, and perhaps not as grim as it sounds. Group exercising and singing is allowed, and you don't have to worry about infecting anyone because they're already infected.

Home has always been a risky place to be confined, particularly for those who lack the luxury of space. Falls and fractures are likely to increase, with a toxic combination of a crowded house, toys and toddlers on the stairs, anger, alcohol and domestic abuse. And an estimated 7,100 people may die prematurely from this home confinement due to poor diet, poverty, inactivity, rickets and suicide. If we focus all our resources and attention on reducing the risk of Covid-19, other equally unpleasant risks may rise up. Child abuse is a major concern.

On the plus side, home confinement is leading to a reduction in pollution, littering, road traffic accidents and dog shit on the pavements (only one a day allowed), and an increase in birdsong and the life expectancy of asthmatics (if they escape the virus). It's beautiful out there without humans.

U-turn if you want to

RISK management in a pandemic is unbelievably complex, trying to balance the deaths due to loss of livelihood, poverty and depression from sending a third of the world's population home to hide, the deaths due to increased waiting times for treatment of urgent non-infectious conditions such as heart disease and cancer, and the rapid number of deaths in a short space of time from Covid-19, which will overload most health services and mortuaries, but not for ever. In such circumstances anyone is allowed to U-turn provided they own up and end up facing in the right direction.

The Chinese did the first U-turn, swiftly followed by the World Health Organization, which reassured us the threat was "moderate" until 30 January, when it was subtly upgraded to "international emergency". Travel instructions were initially confused but it issued clear guidance on the essential protection of healthcare workers and the need to ramp up testing, trace contacts and isolate to break the chain. Enforced social distancing was vital. Britain slept.

The virus is less infectious than, say, measles and less of a killer than Ebola. But when "ebeasles" comes along, we really will be screwed. For now, it's the health and social care workers, and those with bodies weakened by pre-existing disease, who are most at risk.

Survival of the fittest

THE elephant in the room in this pandemic is not just our poor public health response, but our poor public health. The general health of Brits, Americans and other rich nations in general is dire. This pandemic will very likely demonstrate survival of the fittest. If ever there was a time to give up smoking and get fitter, it's now.

Unfit for purpose

THE government's plan A was to promote herd immunity, telling the public that 60-70 percent would likely get it anyway, and mildly, and they'd be doing the sick a favour by licking door handles and lavatory seats to build up herd resistance. Without vaccines, it's a high-risk strategy – like parents who hold measles parties so their kids can catch it "naturally", then run screaming to the NHS when they realise what an unpleasant, even lethal illness it can be (and, like HIV, it came from our conquest of animals).

The big flaw in the herd immunity plan came from the daft idea that 60-70 percent of the UK population are fit and healthy. Many young and middle-aged people have a full house of chronic disease. They were never going to get Covid-19 "mildly" and would die with octogenarians in an overwhelmed NHS, alongside exhausted staff.

Hence the screeching U-turn. Overnight, we went from "catch it now to build up our immunity" to "avoid it at all costs, to stop killing nurses and sick people". Seldom has a message been more confused. The next cunning plan was "voluntary distancing" based on "nuanced messaging". It relied on the British being jolly decent people who willingly do the right thing, if only they could remember what it was.

Ask any doctor

ANY doctor could have told Johnson that voluntary nudging would fail. Patients remember 0-14 percent of what doctors tell them. Many don't follow our advice (hence the staggeringly high rates of chronic disease). Around a third of drugs are taken properly, a third are taken sporadically, and a third are stored in the cupboard under the sink in case of a Soviet invasion.

Humans can resist everything bar temptation. If you tell people they're at very low risk but they shouldn't go to bars, restaurants, cafés and gyms, and then keep them open with their near bankrupt owners' pleading faces staring out, you won't get much compliance.

High-risk, anti-social health behaviour is normalised in the UK. Drink-driving, texting while driving, not vaccinating your kids, smoking with your kids in the car, not washing your hands between shitting, sex and spring rolls, coughing in your doctor's face from two feet, not picking up your dog's poo, etc.

Our public health disaster is a real test for Johnson, who by nature is socially permissive. Until recently he was shaking hands and huddling close to his advisers in briefings. If you want to sell social distancing, you have to follow it too. The non-verbal message was: "I'm saying all this but I don't really mean it."

By the time he finally sounded like he meant it, it was too late for him and it may be two weeks too late for the country. We won't know until the tests are back. If only we were doing them...

Death, but not as we know it

A HOSPITAL during a pandemic is not a peaceful place to die. We need to greatly increase community and home palliative care for those who don't want to be in the queue for intubation. British figures for ICU survival with Covid-19 currently show 66 percent of those intubated have died, so ventilators are saving about one third of severely ill patients, even fewer among the elderly. Better for many to get the best possible end-of-life care at home, which is where we should be putting our resources. When all this is over, we will need to help those recovering after intensive care, and those grieving a death that, because of the risk of infection, was in isolation.

The last laugh?

BORIS JOHNSON may yet have the last laugh if he can keep deaths down to 5,700 without destroying everyone's livelihood. But models are simplistic security blankets for a reality that is far more complex and unpredictable. They can be way off the mark. It could equally be that the virus has the last laugh. Remember, it exists only to replicate, and is even better at its job than Johnson. In the meantime, wash your hands, keep your distance and try to have five portions of fun a day.

---

18 March: Government announces closure of schools. **23 Mar**: PM announces UK lockdown, orders people to stay at home. **25 Mar**: Coronavirus Act 2020 receives royal assent. **26 Mar**: Lockdown measures legally come into force. At 8pm, millions join first "Clap for Carers" tribute to NHS and care workers. **27 Mar**: PM and health secretary test positive for Covid-19.

MD on The great escape?

Private Eye 1520 Press day: 20 April

5,006 daily cases **905** daily deaths **13,037** UK deaths to date

Prime suspect

BORIS JOHNSON was by turns foolish, unlucky and lucky. Foolish because he shook hands in hospitals treating Covid-19 patients and huddled up in press conference and committee rooms with other highly exposed individuals, while supposedly "selling" a policy of social isolation. Unlucky because, at his age, 92 percent of people infected with coronavirus don't need hospitalisation. And lucky because he swiftly got an intensive care bed in a teaching hospital under the care of one of the UK's top respiratory physicians, and escaped intubation by a retired gynaecologist in a repurposed conference centre.

NHS staff are emerging from the crisis with reputations enhanced, particularly Jenny from New Zealand and Luis from Portugal. Johnson less so. Did he take his eye off the virus, juggling Brexit, floods, reshuffle and remarriage? Or did he simply not take it seriously? On 2 March, Imperial College modelling advised that unconstrained spreading could lead to 500,000 deaths. But on 3 March, a fearless Johnson joked about shaking hands with everyone. "Our country remains extremely well prepared. We already have a fantastic NHS, fantastic testing systems and fantastic surveillance of the spread of disease." So are we heading for the most deaths in Europe? Why have so many NHS staff died? And will we ever beat Germany?

Reasons to be cheerful?

FIRST the good news. Personal protective equipment (PPE) aside, the NHS is coping with Covid. Managers have performed miracles in bed availability. Starting from near the bottom of the EU league table for beds and ITU capacity, NHS England cancelled all routine operations and freed up 33,000 hospital beds for coronavirus patients very quickly.

Operating theatres and equipment were requisitioned for Covid-19 ventilation. A 2,000-bed Nightingale hospital in London's Excel centre was built in less than a fortnight, with another at Birmingham's NEC.

Private hospitals have handed over their beds if needed.

The NHS sat tight over Easter weekend, waiting for the massive peak in demand that the government's model had predicted. Covid wards remained busy, other parts of hospitals were eerily quiet; A&E attendances were down 25 percent, and only 19 of the 2,000 Excel beds were occupied. Everyone heaved a huge sigh of relief. Then the latest ONS death figures came in for England and Wales…

Stay at home, die, protect the NHS

NOT only were there 6,000 more deaths in a single week than the average of the previous five years, but half of them weren't linked to Covid-19.

It could be that people are dying from Covid-19 in homes and in care homes, but because we're not testing much in the community it doesn't make it on to the death certificate. Or it could be that people have been so frightened by the "stay at home, save lives" message, and so fearful of catching Covid-19 in hospital, they're not seeking emergency help for heart attacks, strokes, appendicitis, meningitis or sepsis. It may also be that cancellations of clinics and routine treatment have allowed stable conditions to deteriorate.

Consultants complain off the record that their patients have been "thrown under a bus". They just aren't seeing the volume of emergencies they would expect. They're unlikely to have simply stopped happening. Meanwhile, some patients are making it to hospital, but sadly too late. And cancer hasn't gone anywhere. As Professor Karol Sikora puts it: "Around 450 people die every day of cancer in the UK. There is no peak and the numbers aren't coming down. Unless we get control of the situation now, that will increase – potentially up to 60,000 unnecessary fatalities. Cancer is relentless – we need to act."

Even children are dying of various non-Covid conditions, with parents unable to get urgent treatment for them. Simon Stevens, CEO of NHS England, has begged those with serious illness to use the NHS, but for some it's too late. They have been frightened to death.

'Go to work, die, wish you had a better mask'

HEALTH and care staff have been truly heroic in this outbreak, and 65 have already died. Most would swap the Thursday clapping for a properly fitting mask and some eye goggles. Many are still having to

BYO, with the NHS Supply Chain in outsourced chaos. Consultant Peter Greenhouse told MD: "I bought goggles for my team by shopping at Poundland. Our Covid-19 lead nurse rates them highly – comfy close fit, very clear view, good side protection."

Health secretary Matt Hancock has even warned staff not to overuse PPE. As if people are somehow able to get through a 12-hour shift, pumped full of stress and adrenaline, without needing to change gowns for a piss. Now staff are being told to recycle them. It would be funny if so many staff weren't dying.

"It's hard to complain when everyone says they're doing their best, but this is a fucking airborne biological hazard they're exposing us to," one junior doctor told me. "It killed many staff at close range in China and Italy. They can't say they weren't warned or didn't have time to prepare. My PPE has been patchy at best; sometimes it's all there, sometimes it isn't. The fear started to creep in when the first UK death was announced, but now two of our own nurses are being ventilated. There's no such thing as zero risk, but I keep Googling for staff deaths in Germany and I can't find any."

Each death should be reported to the Health and Safety Executive (HSE) for investigation, to determine if it was an avoidable workplace death due to exposure to a biological agent. The government press briefings have been shameful, by turns unable to say how many nurses have died (health secretary Matt Hancock) and then refusing to number all the health and social care staff who had died because it was "inappropriate" (Hancock giving a hospital pass to Ruth May, chief nursing officer for England). A number breaches no one's confidentiality. Hopefully the HSE will leave no stone unturned to determine whether inadequate PPE contributed to death.

Care home conundrum

FOR those in their 80s with a life expectancy of months, spending them in isolation with only *Cash in the Attic* for company is a unique form of torture. BBC News reports of the virus "spreading like wildfire through care homes" are unlikely to lift the mood.

There have been thousands of poorly documented deaths in UK care homes now, and we may never be certain why. Some residents may simply be struggling to understand why everyone is so anxious and scared, why relatives aren't allowed to visit, why staff are wearing aprons, gloves and masks (if they're lucky), and why they have to stay in their rooms when the weather outside is glorious. Like a grief reaction that follows any profound loss, some may just be taking to their beds and giving up. As one resident joked: "If this is all I've got left, I'd rather lick a nurse and get it over with."

Dirty tactics

SEVERE Covid-19 isn't an ordinary viral pneumonia. It's more of a dirty bomb, causing havoc in the immune and vascular systems, with elements of high-altitude pulmonary oedema leaving you fighting for breath. The overwhelming immune reaction can lead to a cytokine storm with widespread thromboembolism, causing clots in the lungs and strokes. Death can be very quick. Alas, the vast majority of older people who get serious disease simply can't be saved. Ventilation currently saves 50 percent, but recovery takes months. And nearly all deaths occur outside ITU. Prevention is clearly far better than cure.

Good deaths are available...

MD has contacted a number of doctors involved in frontline palliative care for patients dying with Covid-19 and the responses have been reassuring. A Covid death for the elderly is usually gentle, well-controlled and quick. More challenging is the separation from relatives and the barrier nursing, but some contact is usually now permitted.

England v Germany (v Italy v Spain)

THE simplest explanation for Germany's lower death tally for both citizens and staff is that they went hard and fast in the basics of infection control – test, trace, isolate, break the chain – as well as social isolation and lockdown. This was combined with a degree of luck. The early outbreak in Germany was largely among younger, fitter citizens who'd come back from skiing holidays and were much more likely to become super-spreaders than die. Testing and isolating brought in huge benefits compared to the UK's sub-optimal approach.

Italy has also done loads of testing, but there the virus hit first in an area full of elderly people with high rates of smoking and air pollution. There were thousands of deaths very quickly, and health services were overwhelmed. ITU doctors were trying to manage 1,200 patients at once and the EU did not exactly spring into action to help them. High-tech healthcare may not have made much difference anyway, as 87 percent of the deaths were in those over 70. Spain was caught cold with Covid after 8,000 early deaths were mistaken for seasonal flu. Pandemic deaths depend on many complex factors, and not just "the government is shit".

The trouser leg of death

ITALY's death total may also have been higher because, in the chaos, just about every death was laid at the door of Covid-19, whereas canny countries are now differentiating between those dying "of" or "with" the disease.

The UK's withdrawal of community testing and easing-off on death certificate procedures means many deaths won't be put down to Covid-19 when perhaps they should be. It's a clever strategy, mixing Covid deaths in with the regular deaths and spreading them out for as long as possible until people cease noticing. It's akin to a prisoner of war losing soil from an escape tunnel down the trouser leg of death. They might have got away with it if the spike in death hadn't been so high. So is it too late to ramp up testing?

Testing times

THE PCR (polymerase chain reaction) test is done via a throat swab that tells you, five days later, if you were shedding virus at the point of swabbing five days previously. Drive through "stay in the car, wind down the window" testing reduces the risk of spread during the swab, but it needs to be easily accessible for all health and care staff, particularly the low paid. Currently it isn't. We need to ramp up testing to track and stop transmission, and hope people aren't too scared, depressed or agoraphobic to leave the house.

The key to unlocking

INFECTION control aims to get the reproduction factor, R0, to less than one. Those infected then pass it on to an average of under one person. You have some control over spread. In the UK, we don't know what the figure is because we don't have sufficient data. In Germany, it's 0.7, and lockdown measures are starting to be lifted this week. Monitoring must continue to stamp out future outbreaks. Jena, the only German city to make face masks compulsory, has recorded no new virus infections in eight days. In the UK, we don't even have enough masks for health and care staff.

Model airplanes

WHY aren't we asking the 15,000 people a day who are still flying into the UK, including those from the US, China, Spain and Italy, to self-isolate for seven days on arrival? Why didn't we do it weeks ago? The only conclusion is that the government's "model" is still one of staged herd immunity without admitting it. It's like one massive, secret measles party.

Over before it began?

PANDEMIC was everyone's number one death threat, and we've had plenty of warnings since SARS in 2003. So why couldn't we stop it?

The first case probably occurred in Wuhan on 17 November, but China took until 8 December to confirm it officially. Wuhan is a very busy national and international travel hub: trains, plains, lorries, cars and shipping. China denied there was human-to-human transmission until 21 January. It did, however, start bulk-buying masks, PPE and ventilators on the global market. On 23 January, Wuhan was put into lockdown, followed by Hubei. But already in 2020, 17 passenger flights had flown directly from Wuhan to the UK, and 614 flights from the whole of China. No one was checked on arrival.

"We're following the science of gut instinct"

On 19 February, there were two deaths in Iran and one in Italy. Dozens of flights were coming in and out of the UK from both countries unchecked, and thousands of UK residents were holidaying and skiing in Italy.

The northern Italian outbreak suddenly mushroomed. The UK government threw in the towel on virus suppression. The Germans put their towels down early and everywhere. They knew the pandemic couldn't be stopped, but they believed it could be suppressed. They protected their citizens and staff better than us, their children are going back to school, their key industries are opening and their meticulous testing continues. If only…

Know your numbers

HERD immunity is simple. You either live or die. The UK government has decided to run with the herd. If we don't invent a vaccine, most of us will eventually get Covid-19, if suicide, cancer and heart disease don't get us first. So then what would be your chances of survival?

The *Lancet* has published figures from China, which may need to be taken with a pinch of sanitiser, of age-related risks of hospitalisation and death, once you know you're infected.

The age-related deaths curve for Covid-19 – rising from a 0.0016 percent risk of dying for those aged 0-9 to a 7.8 percent risk among the over-80s – almost perfectly mirrors your age-related risk of dying from all causes over a year. So the coronavirus outbreak is compressing a year's worth of death risk into a few months. If you can live with that, you'll survive after lockdown.

Count ourselves lucky

IN 2016, Tom Koch, a Canadian epidemiologist, predicted a major pandemic of a new and untreatable infection within eight years. It would affect 60 percent of the global population and have a mortality rate of 30-35 percent.

We can count ourselves extremely lucky that for Covid-19 the overall mortality rate is predicted to be around 0.34-1 percent in developed countries. But it could be far higher in the poorest, where millions already die each year from TB, malnutrition, diarrhoeal diseases, malaria, measles, polluted air and water, and smoking. The

UK has blagged an extra 60 ventilators from Germany. The Central African Republic has three ventilators for a population of 5m. They need Covid-19 like a hole in the lungs.

QALY folly?

IT's perhaps tasteless to consider value for money during a deadly pandemic, but that's what the National Institute for Health and Care Excellence (NICE) was set up to do, and it deemed we could only afford treatments for any disease of up to £25,000 per quality adjusted life year (QALY).

When the final reckoning is done on this pandemic, including the costs to the economy and treating all the neglected diseases, we may end up spending millions per life saved. Or there may be no sum net gain in lives saved at all. Contrary to chancellor Rishi Sunak's promise, money has always been an object for the NHS. If you don't have it, you can't pay for it.

Living with risk

NOTHING lasts for ever, neither life nor lockdown. Covid-19 looks hardier than the 2003 SARS and may hang round for years in some form or other. We can't hide indoors for ever. We live with complex and dangerous global risks every day. The air we breathe is so polluted it kills 7m people a year, mainly innocent bystanders. Tobacco kills another 8m, including 1.2m innocents from passive smoking, a fair proportion of them children. Covid-19 is just another in a long line of life-threatening risks humans have made and are having to manage. They all deserve urgent attention, and that starts with understanding that we are all connected. No risk is an island.

Exit strategy

"THE single most important thing we can do for the health of our economy is to protect the health of our people," promised the chancellor. "It's not a case of choosing between the economy and public health." And yet that is what the Tories have done since 2010.

One reason we've had so many younger Covid-19 deaths is because we have appalling levels of chronic disease. That's why herd immunity was so risky, and why public health experts are up in arms. When we finally emerge from the pandemic, every country must make the health and wellbeing of people and planet their paramount political concern. The same resolve that's gone into fighting coronavirus must fight, say, child malnutrition (5m deaths a year) and suicide (1m deaths).

As my GP trainer, Dr Brian Clarke, used to say: "The most powerful drug in the world is kindness. It works for everyone, it's very hard to get the dose wrong, and it's free at the point of delivery." If we seriously want to stop the next pandemic, we need to start being kinder to animals. And yet the live animal markets in Wuhan have reopened...

---

2 April: Government to carry out 100,000 coronavirus tests by end of April, says health secretary Matt Hancock. Government publishes advice to care homes. Some patients "may have Covid-19, whether symptomatic or asymptomatic. All of these patients can be safely cared for in care homes if the guidance is followed." It also states: "Negative tests are not required prior to transfers/admissions into the care home." **5 Apr:** PM Boris Johnson admitted to hospital after coronavirus symptoms persist. **6 Apr:** PM put in intensive care. Government admits none of its 17.5m coronavirus antibody tests work. **9 Apr:** UK records 938 deaths in 24 hours, highest daily tally so far. PM moved from intensive care. **11 Apr:** To complaints that NHS workers don't have correct PPE, home secretary Priti Patel says she's "sorry if people feel there have been failings". **12 Apr:** PM discharged from hospital. **15 Apr:** Prior testing before discharge to care homes becomes mandatory (er, where available).

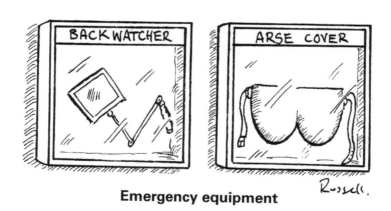

Emergency equipment

MD on The UK plays catch-up

Private Eye 1521   Press day: 4 May

5,006 daily cases   **520** daily deaths   **28,490** UK deaths to date

Lose-lose scenario

PANDEMIC planning is the ultimate lose-lose scenario. The lives and livelihoods lost from the virus have to be balanced against the lives and livelihoods lost from the "treatment". This virus is causing a surge of deaths particularly in the sick and elderly, whereas lockdown is causing a smaller surge in non-Covid deaths and a steady, sustained increase in harm to those who have their whole lives ahead of them.

Brutally put, children are being harmed to save adults; the poor are being harmed more than the rich; and some people have become so conditioned to "stay at home" that not even a medical emergency will tempt them to seek help. But if we didn't lock down, the NHS could be so overwhelmed with Covid that those with non-Covid diseases would also die. It's a Catch-a-virus 22.

Given such staggering complexity, the best one can hope for overall is "harm minimisation". To achieve that, experts from all disciplines must subject their models and data on the benefits and harms of any strategy to full public scrutiny. And politicians need to admit their errors in real time. It has taken more than three months to move from Patient Zero to mass testing and tracing. It would be churlish not to welcome Matt Hancock's 100,000 tests a day (even though they included requests and promptly fell again), but thousands more lives might have been saved by earlier action. It is time for an apology.

Meanwhile, after mothballing London's little-used Nightingale hospital, questions will be asked about the money and resources spent on it. But it's worth noting that the NHS needs extra capacity (and staff) in case there's a second spike in infection.

Cheer Korea

THE first thing a South Korean friend in London did when she got wind of the coronavirus outbreak in January was to buy and wear a mask. MD thought it an overreaction. The next thing she did was fly home.

How foolish, flying towards the outbreak, MD thought.

Thus far, a country of more than 50m people has recorded 10,793 cases with 9,183 recovered and just 250 deaths, zero current community spread and no ruinous lockdown. They even pulled off an election, with 30m citizens voting in person, without any outbreak. The locked-down UK has had around 40,000 Covid-19 deaths in a population of 65m, with thousands more to follow from collateral damage and unintended consequences. If the UK has been "following the science every step of the way" – as the government insists – what has South Korea been following?

No secret

SOUTH Korea had enough previous experience of SARS and MERS (Middle East respiratory syndrome) outbreaks to know that unless you get a grip immediately, you will forever be playing catch-up. Unchecked, a single SARS-CoV-2 infection can spread to nearly 60,000 people over ten cycles.

So it urgently put in place a system to mask, screen, detect, isolate, contact trace and quarantine contacts, using random temperature checks and mobile phone tracking – as well as credit card and bank record tracking and security camera ID – sacrificing a measure of privacy for the public good, but avoiding the need for extreme lockdown. Since the virus is silently infectious up to five days before symptoms appear, all contacts were traced back for the five days prior to symptoms.

This required strong leadership, good communication and a largely compliant public. Huge resources went into the discovery and roll-out of a PCR swab test. Hundreds of lab facilities were urgently sequestered, as part of a well-funded and coordinated health system that could deliver both preventative public health measures and high-tech treatments.

In the UK, a third of patients admitted to hospital with Covid-19 are dying, as are half those admitted to intensive care. Thousands more deaths are occurring at home, particularly care homes. Was this inevitable and part of the plan? Or have we got some things wrong?

Masks for all?

COUNTRIES where citizens queue for masks at the first whiff of an infectious outbreak tend to have fewer deaths. This does not prove that wearing masks in public reduces the spread of infection (the evidence takes a while to collate), but it's a cultural signifier that a country takes a pandemic seriously, and provides individual reassurance that you are doing all you can to protect yourself and others.

In hospital, many doctors resisted the order to be "bare below the elbows" to reduce the risk of hospital-acquired infection, because the evidence was unclear. But an infectious outbreak is one situation where you have to act quickly, *before* the evidence arrives. The only side effect of a mask is wearing it too high so it obscures your eyesight, and the risk of ridicule.

Likewise, shaming those who don't wear masks is unhelpful. Given the shortage of PPE, citizens would have to make their own, and a family of seven in a cramped flat may struggle to wash and dry their cloth masks three times a day.

Poor prevention

IT's no surprise rich countries with high death tolls from Covid-19 are generally poor at prevention. The UK and US didn't initially take the virus seriously enough, but nor do they take public health and care of the elderly seriously enough. They both have high levels of income and social inequality, a strong aversion to a nanny state, threadbare social care and a diet of more than 50 percent cheap, sugary, ultra-processed foods.

Most premature deaths from Covid-19 are happening in those with pre-existing chronic disease often related to poor diet and obesity (metabolic syndrome, type 2 diabetes, high blood pressure, heart disease, fatty liver, kidney disease). If the government wants to reduce premature deaths from Covid-19, it needs to improve preventative health all round.

Variable reproduction

IRONICALLY lockdown is likely making chronic disease control even worse (less exercise, more alcohol, worse diet, more stress, more depression, less sleep), and again will disproportionately affect poor people, who are more likely to be living in cramped and crowded conditions where isolation from someone with the virus is near impossible.

The government talks about the need to keep the Reproduction Number (R0) under one, so each infected person passes the virus on to less than one other. But the R0 varies enormously with wealth. Two occupants of a spacious house with a garden will have a far lower R0 than 10 occupants of a tenth-floor flat. Unsurprisingly, the Covid-19 death rate in poor areas is more than double that in wealthy areas.

Hurting children

THE media gave huge coverage to a tiny number of children who became seriously ill with a rare disease that may be linked in some cases to Covid-19. Yet thousands of children are suffering long-term harm from lockdown. There are no documented cases of a child under ten passing Covid-19 to an adult, and many documented cases of children missing vaccination appointments and presenting late to hospital with serious illness, causing avoidable harm and even death.

Social isolation is leading to increased anxiety and probable self-harm, and an increase in child and domestic abuse. Services that normally protect children – educational, social and health – are either unavailable or harder to access. Child and adolescent mental health services have reduced or suspended assessment and treatment clinics in many parts of the UK at precisely the time children and young people are experiencing greater anxiety and depression.

By the time children are allowed back to school, the gap between the haves and have-nots will be even wider. Some parents relish reading with their children; others find it impossible. Those left behind may never catch up. Time to cautiously reopen schools.

Learn not blame

"TO err is human, to cover up is unforgivable, and to fail to learn is inexcusable." So observed Sir Liam Donaldson, a former chief medical officer in England and a founder of the patient safety movement. While NHS staff have it drilled into them about the importance of owning up to error in real time, and the legal duty to report situations that aren't safe, the political culture is the antithesis: never admit error or weakness; cover up as long as possible. This chasm in cultures is vast, and the virus is sailing up the middle. Pandemic errors can't be kicked into the long grass.

Part of the plan?

THE government insists it has followed the science every step of the way, which gives it a convenient scapegoat if the number of deaths reaches unelectable numbers. For now, a slightly careworn Boris Johnson insists everything is going according to a carefully coordinated plan. It seems the failure to get a grip on the pandemic early on was not a serious error of judgement but a deliberate ploy, based on the reasoning that it couldn't be stopped, a drug or vaccine was unlikely to make a huge difference in the next 18 months, so better to get it over with.

Dreaded lurgy

THE relentless focus on the horror of Covid-19 has, as MD predicted, caused much collateral damage and unintended consequences.

Many people have now become fearful to venture outdoors, even if the risks they face by staying put are greater than the risk the infection poses. In the West Midlands, 300 people would not let an ambulance take them to hospital even though a paramedic had triaged their symptoms and declared they needed emergency treatment.

Small wonder the presentation of heart attacks and strokes at hospitals has fallen. People are too frightened to go there. And yet many emergency departments and non-Covid wards are now so empty your chance of any hospital-acquired infection is as low as it's ever been. Indeed, NHS staff twiddling their thumbs should be redeployed to care homes, where the Covid-19 frontline has always been.

Conspiracy theories add to the dread risk, as does the large number of deaths in a short period, akin to a terror attack. Likewise, excess non-

Covid deaths may take longer to manifest, but may well outnumber Covid deaths. The modelling and data for both sides of the government strategy need to be seen and scrutinised to stop us doing more harm than good. Yet they remain secret.

Testing U-turn

A MONTH is a long time in a pandemic. The UK government has gone from confidently declaring that widespread testing for coronavirus was "not an appropriate intervention" to fervently (and correctly) advocating mass testing. This delay cost lives.

When China released the coronavirus genetic code on 12 January, providing a blueprint for a PCR (polymerase chain reaction) swab test to detect the presence of the virus, the UK was one of the first countries to develop it. The UK government started community testing and contact tracing at the start of the pandemic but as cases began to rise, and when infection control was most needed, it was abandoned.

The advice of the World Health Organization to "test, test, test" was, according to Jenny Harries, England's deputy chief medical officer, apparently intended for countries that were "less developed than Britain". In fact, this was nothing to do with "following the science", but simply because we didn't have the capacity to test at scale. Thousands died as we gave up on the basics. At last we are starting to catch up.

No perfect test

MANY countries only do testing in full protective gear because to get a sufficient sample on a naso-pharyngeal throat swab usually causes a gag or cough that risks aerosol spread of the virus. As we are short of PPE, there's a real risk that those doing swabs may become infected.

As swab testing is rolled out, it is being outsourced to private companies employing low paid workers with minimal training. Perhaps not the best recipe for doing the swab properly and not infecting yourself in the process. Self-swabbing is safer but still unpleasant, and only useful if it is done properly. Just as important are the human resources put into specialist contact tracing afterwards. The results don't always match the symptoms and nuanced, specialist interpretation is often needed.

In an ideal world, every positive test would mean you had coronavirus and every negative test would mean you didn't. Alas, the PCR (polymerase chain reaction) test has a false negative rate of up to one in three, so if a patient is truly positive for the virus, there is up to a one in three chance the PCR swab test will come back negative. Even if you swab all hospital patients before returning them to their care homes, some will still be carrying the virus.

The same applies to care home staff. And the virus starts spreading five days before symptoms appear. So it's very difficult to keep it out of care homes completely, particularly when patients require intimate care and there are staff and PPE shortages. But we could have tried a lot harder.

Protecting staff

SOME staff should not be on the frontline because their risk profile is too high. BAME staff may be at both increased genetic risk and cultural risk. Surveys show they find it harder to speak up or be heard when they have safety issues. They also tend to live in multi-generational households. Many are poorly paid and can't afford the luxury of staying safe at home without protected wages. And yet eight out of ten care workers aren't paid at all if they self-isolate.

MD also knows of staff at very high risk who are overriding all concerns and turning up for frontline care out of a sense of vocation and duty – which makes it all the more vital they have the right PPE.

PPE cover-up

WHEN the government realised it didn't have enough PPE despite repeated promises that it did, the Department of Health and Social Care (DHSC) should have apologised. Instead it took steps to remove Covid-19 from the high consequence infectious diseases (HCID) list on 13 March, and downgraded the PPE guidance so less would be needed.

As the BBC's *Panorama* reported, the billion-plus items of PPE the government has supplied included cleaning products and individually counted gloves; gowns, visors, swabs and body bags were not included in the pandemic stockpile; only 12m of the specified 33m FFP3 respirator masks were distributed.

Deaths in service

THE government has announced £60,000 death-in-service payouts for health and care staff, but proving death was work related or linked to inadequate PPE will be very hard as the virus is prevalent everywhere. There would need to be a statistically significant difference in risk in Covid-19 deaths between, say, BAME citizens in general and those working in health and social care, or between comparable groups of frontline doctors and desktop lawyers.

It has emerged that most staff deaths won't automatically go to coroners' inquests, prompting outrage among representative bodies. It would, however, be instructive to compare, for example, whether the large numbers of Filipino health and social care workers who have died in the UK have also died in large number in countries with better provided-for PPE. MD would suspect not.

Care homes

EVEN the most successful countries such as Germany have had outbreaks in care homes. But in the UK there was no swift sharing of NHS infection control expertise and equipment for care staff. How successful that would have been is impossible to say, but the early impression was of a plan to protect the NHS and leave care homes to it.

Rather belatedly, care home staff and residents are being offered tests. They also need to be part of a standardised, coordinated National Health and Care Service.

Peaks and troughs

GOVERNMENTS exist to keep the people safe or, failing that, to lose as few lives as possible. In an average year in the UK there are 600,000 deaths, and not even Nye Bevan could stop them. In general, the older you are the more likely you are to die. Not all deaths from Covid-19 are an avoidable tragedy. If MD was 84 and with dementia, I might welcome the merciful release of a quick Covid death.

In years where the death toll rises, such as the 50,000 excess deaths in 2017-18, a mixture of poverty, extreme temperatures and infectious disease accounts for most. Covid-19 alone may account for 50,000 excess deaths or more, by compressing a whole year's worth of death risk for each of us into a few months; but as with most respiratory outbreaks it disproportionately affects those already in other high-risk groups. As some of those who die from Covid-19 would have died from other causes later in the year, a large spike in deaths during the pandemic is likely to be followed by a fall in expected deaths afterwards.

---

16 April: Lockdown extended. War veteran and charity fundraiser Tom Moore, 99, completes 100 laps of his garden. **20 Apr**: Number of Covid-19 patients in hospital begins to fall in Scotland, Wales and every region of England. **23 Apr**: Human testing for a Covid-19 vaccine begins in Oxford. Donald Trump suggests coronavirus might be treated by injecting disinfectant into the body. **27 Apr**: PM returns to work. **30 April**: PM claims the UK is "past the peak" of Covid-19. **1 May**: Hancock says UK has capacity for 100,000 Covid-19 PCR tests a day. **3 May**: NHS contact tracing app trialled on the Isle of Wight.

"You'll have to speak up, I'm on the train.
Test and trace, you say?"

MD on Risk in the time of corona

Private Eye 1522 **Press day: 18 May**

2,965 daily cases **296** daily deaths **33,966** UK deaths to date

Staying alive

GOOD news. Thus far, 999 out of 1,000 Brits have not died of Covid-19, or as a side effect of lockdown. However, there have still been around 60,000 excess deaths above the five-year norm. It's impossible to say how many of these could have been avoided with, say, a more competent government Covid strategy, and for how long.

In the week to 1 May in England and Wales, the largest number of Covid-19 deaths was in those aged 90 and over (1,494 deaths). In the 80-84 age group, there were 1,096 Covid deaths. Given that the average life expectancy in the UK is 81.25 years and the average life expectancy in a care home is two years even without Covid-19, shielding residents was never going to result in a plethora of quality-adjusted life years. However, not to have tried harder gives the impression of abandoning the most vulnerable and suggests their lives have less worth. The government may not be forgiven for its failure to provide protective equipment for staff and meticulously test those moving in and out of care homes from the outset, when it was clear this was where the greatest risk of death resided.

The bottom line

THERE is no such thing as zero risk, just sensible risk management. There are currently three ways to reduce your risk of dying from Covid-19.

The first is not to catch the virus. The second is to make yourself as healthy as possible so that if you do catch it, you're far more likely to recover fully. And the third is to seek help if you do get seriously ill, whatever the cause. Covid-19 mimics many other illnesses, and people have delayed seeking help for fear of catching it when they already had it.

Currently a third of Covid-19 hospital patients die, and half of those who have been ventilated, so avoiding the infection is preferable, particularly if you're over 50. Outdoors is usually safer than indoors during a respiratory pandemic. Most people get infected in their homes, and lockdown can spread as well as slow infection. But can we now escape without causing even more harm?

Fergie time

THE easing of lockdown based on "good, solid British common sense" and "alertness" may yet be a joyful affair. Boris Johnson is still trying to sell the chart-topping 60,000 excess deaths thus far as a success, because lockdown has apparently saved 450,000 lives based on "the reasonable worst-case scenario" of 510,000 deaths without it.

That scarily precise number was based on modelling and guesswork by Imperial College's Professor Neil Ferguson, who invited his lover to travel across the most infected city in the UK to break the rules he had helped devise. This suggests either he doesn't truly believe his own estimates, or he believes it's OK for informed individuals to make their own nuanced interpretation of lockdown laws. Experts use common sense, so why shouldn't everyone?

This may have given Johnson the excuse he needed to ease lockdown and pass the buck for the consequences on to the good sense of the notoriously alert British public. They might spot a lover illegally entering a professor's house at dusk, but a 10-micron respiratory droplet is a much tougher ask. "Stay apart" makes a lot more sense than "Stay alert".

Herd around the world

ONE hope for our "late lockdown, give up on testing and abandon border control" plan was that such a high number of "round one" deaths would also mean a high number of infections in the community, and put us well on the way to herd immunity as we exit lockdown.

Alas, a seroprevalence study of more than 60,000 people in Spain, which like the UK has a high death toll, has found that overall only 5 percent of the population had antibodies to the SARS-CoV-2 virus. Even in Madrid – the region with the largest outbreak – it rose to just 11 percent. Figures in many other countries are similar, suggesting the virus may be travelling around the world for a few years before anything like herd immunity develops, or a vaccine or drug stops it.

Risk in perspective

THERE is often a big gap between someone's perceived risk of a threat and the actual risk. When a risk receives relentless media attention, it inflates its true risk and leads to harmful decisions. So fear of catching Covid-19 in hospital may dissuade people from seeking help for life-threatening conditions, including Covid-19.

Because of the high excess death toll, mistakes made in care homes and general lack of trust in the government, it may be impossible to convince some parents, pupils, teachers and workers it's safe to go back to school or work. Others (particularly young men) see themselves as invincible and will take full advantage of their new freedom to take insane risks like, say, teaching themselves to surf while drunk in turbulent seas devoid of lifeguard patrols.

Age-related risk

IN an ideal world, people's level of fear and anxiety would be proportional to the risk they face. The age-related risk of death by Covid-19 for people who do not currently have it (the population fatality rate), based on data from England and Wales up to 1 May, is:

Age 0-14: 1 in 5,337,266
15-24: 1 in 279,550
25-44: 1 in 44,423
45-64: 1 in 4,388
65-74: 1 in 1,143
75-90: 1 in 225
90+: 1 in 81

For those under 14, the chance of death from Covid-19 is negligible (you are far more likely to be killed by lightning this year). We still aren't sure how likely children are to pass the virus on to adults, but it might be safer for them to be at school than shut at home all day with grandad. Men have roughly double the risk of getting the virus and dying, compared with women of the same age. Fatal risk doubles for each 6–7 years of extra age: an 80-year-old has around 500 times the risk of dying from Covid-19 than a 20-year-old. This disease, like death itself, is very ageist.

How not to catch it

HOW successful the government's new-found zest for "test, treat, isolate and quarantine at the borders" is remains to be seen. The fact that we've eased lockdown before finding out suggests our own actions are still far more likely to protect us from the virus than the government's.

Fortunately, SARS viruses aren't that easy to catch. In 2003, one SARS outbreak was traced to eight people in the Metropole hotel in Hong Kong, but all on the same floor. It required close contact to spread. The equation is simple: successful infection = exposure to virus x time. The highest-risk environments will clearly be enclosed, with a high density of people present for long periods with poor/recycled air circulation: homes, care homes, nursing homes, planes, prisons, call centres, warehouses, factories and religious ceremonies.

Coughing and sneezing are not the only viral accelerants. Loud equipment that obliges workers to yell at one other spreads the virus. Singing in a choir spreads the virus, even with social distancing. In most circumstances, a metre apart is low-risk; 2m even more so.

Well spaced, well ventilated offices are low-risk. Just about everything is safer outdoors. Even if a cyclist or runner gets in your grill, you generally need at least five minutes of close contact to contract. Viral droplets land on surfaces, so regular hand-washing and not touching your face remain as important as ever.

A mask may prevent you passing the virus on, rather than prevent you inhaling it, but if you leave it on the sideboard it can be a vector for infection.

"Ah, I'll miss the birdsong when the traffic's back"

How to reduce risk of death if you get it

THE infection fatality rate (ie the risk of dying if you do get the virus) also increases steeply with age. You can't do much about that but, like just about every other disease, you can reduce your risk of death at any age by being as healthy as you can.

Ninety-five percent of those dying from Covid-19 in hospital have underlying health conditions. Dementia, obesity, type 2 diabetes, high blood pressure, cancer, kidney, heart and lung disease were all associated with substantial increases in Covid death.

Given that 80 percent of the chronic diseases that kill us prematurely can be prevented by a healthy lifestyle, and many pose a much greater risk than Covid-19, the government had a golden opportunity to improve public health while it had the nation's attention. Eat well, avoid sugar, be physically active, manage your mental health, sleep well. Instead, it became absorbed in a single health risk to the exclusion of others. Imprisoning children in the passive smoke of their relatives, eating sugary rubbish, not moving from their screens, and spreading virus around the house is a recipe for disaster.

Getting risk wrong

THE UK government has finally admitted that abandoning "test, trace, isolate" early on was due to a lack of testing capacity, rather than good science. Former health secretary Jeremy Hunt was keen to deflect blame from the, er, former health secretary, declaring it to be one of the "biggest failures of scientific advice to ministers in our lifetimes". His replacement, Matt Hancock, then claimed the government had "tried to throw a protective ring around care homes right from the outset". Thousands of care homeowners, staff and residents would beg to differ. Contrast this to the honesty of NHS staff in owning up to errors:

● "Politicians and NHS England shout the orders but it was NHS staff that discharged patients to care homes, often without testing or waiting for the test result to come back. Sure, there was a shortage of PCR tests and a lot of pressure to clear the decks and discharge, but we're supposed to be advocates of patients and the experts in infection control. We should have kept them in isolation until they had a negative test result. It wouldn't have stopped every case, but it certainly would have helped." – *An infection control sister*

- "We isolated a local GP practice and turned it into a red 'Covid only hot-hub', and paid GPs £900 a session to work there. I did three sessions without seeing a single patient. We belatedly switched to home visiting and discovered many frightened people had just sat at home with serious illness – both Covid and non-Covid – and some died." – *A GP*

- "There has been a medical overreaction to C19, to counter the government's underreaction. It's true that uncontrolled Covid puts up waiting lists for everything else, but we had no plan to counter this. 7 million are now on the waiting list for other diseases. Most units have stopped renal transplantation and the workup of the next lot of transplants. Patients who were about to get a living transplant before dialysis have been slipping on to dialysis unnecessarily. Other units have plodded on and others have done very illogical things, such as putting a curtain between the 'dirty' and 'clean' parts of their ward and kept transplanting. There is huge variability, no coherent plan, and non-Covid patients are paying the price. We have run out of drugs like EPO [erythropoietin] and oncology colleagues have run out of chemo and radioactive materials for radiotherapy. All routine endoscopy has stopped. How many early cancers on a two-week wait have been made worse by the delay? The 'first three diagnoses are Covid' mantra is rife, and patients with very treatable acute serious disease – eg asthma – are being left 12-18 hours before somebody sensible realises the wheeze is not C19 and they need nebulisers etc." – *A nephrologist*

- "It seems poor form to question Nightingale hospitals, but none have emergency departments and transferring patients always meant sparing staff and equipment the NHS couldn't spare. Patients are often obese, have micro-blood clots everywhere and multi-organ problems, and yet the criteria for our Nightingale hospital was BMI <35 and single organ failure. So virtually no patients were eligible for transfer anyway and it quickly became a massive white elephant. We knew this early on, so why did we open 12 of them, other than for a costly PR stunt?" – *An ITU doctor*

- "The lack of PPE has at times been scandalous, but so has our failure to prevent staff who were clearly at high risk (older, male, BAME, pre-existing conditions, etc) from working on the Covid frontline. They should not have been allowed to. It was appalling risk management by the NHS." – *An NHS manager*

Right second time?

ALL countries are at risk of a second wave of infection. Testing alone is not the answer: the government needs a well-resourced network of contact tracing to squash a second wave and provide real-time regional data on infection control. The national R number is far less useful than knowing what is going on in your community. Those in high-risk environments (factories, call centres, schools, hospitals, nursing homes, public transport) need to be screened and tested regularly to provide evidence of safety. This risk is a complex mixture of viral evolution, human behaviour and government mandate. Microbes often outsmart human attempts to control them, hence the millions of deaths from antibiotic resistance. But risk is also part of being alive. In 1995, UCL academic John Adams argued that everyone has a "risk thermostat", set at a level they feel comfortable with. But circumstances force the setting to change. "In the dance of the risk thermostats, the music never stops."' So keep dancing, preferably outside.

---

5 May: UK passes Italy with Europe's highest declared death toll. **7 May:** Bank of England predicts UK economy will shrink 14% in 2020. **10 May:** PM unveils new "stay alert" slogan, announces a conditional plan to lift lockdown, and says people who can't work from home should return to the workplace but avoid public transport. **11 May:** Government advises people in England to wear face coverings in enclosed spaces where social distancing is not possible. Teaching unions say plans to reopen schools on 1 June are "reckless".

MD on Test, trace and trust

Private Eye 1523   Press day: 1 June

1,905 daily cases   **172** daily deaths   **37,531 UK** deaths to date

The Arse number

THERE'S a good reason people with symptoms, and those living with them, are asked to stay put in a pandemic. A single infection can eventually spread to thousands. We were late to lockdown in London, but areas of low infectivity could still be protected if no outsider travelled to them.

By driving his family from London to Durham, Dominic Cummings risked spreading the virus to a less exposed community, particularly as his family needed to access the local NHS, where spread commonly occurs. And spread to hospitals can spread to care homes. Cummings' behaviour plausibly harmed people in an area 260 miles from his home, and the infection rate in the North-east is now much higher.

Cummings knew perfectly well in advance how reckless his behaviour was, and didn't ask for advice before he left. He knows he would have been ordered to stay in London and offered help with future childcare should he need it. The least he could do is apologise to people in the North-east. By refusing to accept he has done anything wrong, he is behaving like a modern-day Typhoid Mary and encouraging others to copy him. Taking the virus cross-country can be disastrous, as can driving for five hours without a break and driving to test visual impairment.

If everyone returned to work when their closest colleague had tested positive and their partner had symptoms, took their highly infectious family cross-country for better childcare options and visited a local beauty spot to test their eyesight, the R number would be off the scale. Just don't.

Backtrack and trace

THREE months after assuring us mass testing was only for developing countries, the government has finally launched its test, trace and isolate programme. It's important but not the only answer. It only traces contacts of symptomatic people with a positive test, missing false negatives (30 percent) and all those spreading the virus without symptoms. And crucially it relies on trust.

Health secretary Matt Hancock is now playing his "civic duty" card but has become hard to take seriously. Stay at home was "the law", "an order" and "an instruction" under lockdown: "If one person breaks the rules, we will all suffer." Hancock was "incandescent with rage" at the frolics of chief lockdown modeller Professor Neil Ferguson, declaring it to be "a matter for the police". Dominic Cummings, by contrast, was simply "safeguarding potential future childcare needs" and "acting within the guidelines", according to Hancock (but guilty of "three clear breaches of lockdown" according to Hancock's predecessor, Jeremy Hunt).

Under the new rules, contacts who were within two metres of a positive case for 15 minutes or more in the 48 hours before symptoms developed will be asked to quarantine at home for 14 days. Will they comply when Cummings didn't? Compliance is also likely to be hampered by software glitches, delays in getting tests back, confusing communication and a lack of personnel and coordination. The "essential" phone tracing app is not fully functional, testing has been outsourced privately with no connection to primary care, and contact tracers at home and in call centres speak of a "fiasco". Track and trace should have been tried and tested before easing lockdown.

Latest data

HOW many of the daily positive coronavirus cases are effectively tracked and traced remains to be seen. The UK is currently second (behind Spain) in the excess deaths per million league table (891). Data from the Office for National Statistics suggests that only 7 percent of people (around 4m) have been infected in England, making herd immunity without a vaccine a pipe dream.

SAGE v Independent SAGE

INDEPENDENT SAGE is a group of scientists set up to mirror the government's Scientific Advisory Group on Emergencies (SAGE), but with more public health expertise and less Dominic Cummings. It believes it is too early to ease lockdown and open schools, and that most of the UK's 60,000 excess deaths could have been avoided with a competent pandemic plan, rather than late lockdown, zero border control and delayed test and trace.

This has forced the hand of SAGE, with two members – Prof John Edmunds and Sir Jeremy Farrar – also declaring that: "The science is clear it is too early to lift lockdown." SAGE has also released documents which might explain the state we're in. SAGE estimates only half of people who develop coronavirus symptoms self-isolate for at least a week. And that was pre-Cummings.

Care home chaos

MANY countries failed to protect care homes. The UK policy of emptying NHS hospitals by discharging patients back to care homes who were carrying the virus was very poor infection control. Matt Hancock claims he "threw a protective ring around care homes" from the outset, but that is clearly untrue.

The government's own guidance on the admission of residents, from 2 April, states some "may have Covid-19, whether symptomatic or asymptomatic. All of these patients can be safely cared for in care homes if the guidance is followed." It also states that "negative tests are not required prior to transfers/admissions into the care home".

After the last issue (1522) reported an infection control sister's view that NHS staff should have defied government orders and refused to discharge patients to care homes until they'd had a negative test, two care home managers contacted the *Eye*. One tried to refuse the entry of a hospital patient who did not have a negative test, but was told he had no authority to stop the discharge and the patient was *en route* back

to him already. Another gave a different view: "The care home system operates on very fine profit margins, and money follows the residents. If we refused entry to anyone who didn't have a negative test for Covid-19, we'd all be bankrupt. As it turns out, so many residents have died, many care homes will go bankrupt anyway."

A new study of care homes in west London has found that a quarter of residents died in two months (a mortality increase of more than 200 percent). Forty percent of residents were infected and more than 40 percent of those had no symptoms. To get a grip in care homes, everyone needs testing.

Lockdown in jail

PRISONS are another hotbed of Covid spread. A prison nurse has told the *Eye*: "Social distancing is near impossible and medical facilities are an afterthought in older prisons, so we struggle along in overcrowded rooms with inadequate PPE. Prison officers have been given the right masks (without any proper fitting) and cheerfully administer medication to those in need using pots of water passed down the whole line, thereby making an excellent reservoir available to everyone queuing to cough or splutter over. Anyone with a cough or runny nose, or inmates who fake a cough to escape solitary confinement, are immediately referred to me as a potential Covid case.

"Unsurprisingly, drug use has increased, and the risks of opioid and spice overdose. Ambu-bags that hand pump air into the lungs are prohibited (and removed from emergency bags) due to the risk of aerosol contamination. All we're left with is Naloxone, which can reverse overdose if you're quick enough, or the dreadful scenario of waiting for cardiac arrest to occur, and trying chest compressions only."

Gimme shelter

SHELTERED accommodation is also a high-risk environment that has had little attention. As one resident in Northumberland put it: "Many of us have cognitive impairment and don't get social distancing. We have to share washing machines. Some residents have carers coming in every day. Many are dependent on their families to deliver food. There is a constant stream of people delivering supermarket shopping, medication, mail and Amazon orders. Everyone touches the same stair rails, lift controls, fire doors and buttons to open the automatic external doors. I have never seen anyone cleaning any of these. Residents try to go up and down stairs without touching the rails, which sounds like a recipe for falls."

Ask for help sooner?

WHEN should you stay at home with symptoms, and when should you seek urgent help? Covid-19 has turned out to be a highly unpredictable multi-system disease. Some people – "the happy hypoxics" – can have critically low oxygen saturation levels but appear relatively well. Patients can also deteriorate very quickly with no warning, having previously appeared to make good progress. In hospital, they have a 70 percent chance of recovery; at home they usually die. Would more have survived if they'd got hospital care more quickly?

As one relative put it: "My dad died from Covid-19 on Tuesday. He was 60 years old with no known health conditions aside from slightly high blood pressure. He stayed at home with severe flu symptoms for almost two weeks because we thought it would be like flu, and that he would recover. He was taken to hospital when he became confused, lost his balance and his speech became slurred.

"When he got to hospital, he tested positive for Covid-19, had suffered a heart attack and had a bleed on his brain. Over three days his breathing deteriorated until he was eventually ventilated. A few hours later he went into renal failure and all support was withdrawn. His final hours were peaceful and dignified but what preceded them was terrifying and traumatic. Such a horrific way to die. I wonder whether it would have made a difference if we sought help earlier? People need to understand what this virus can do to relatively young, healthy people and seek help."

A pathologist shouts...

"MANY pathologists warned that a pandemic was inevitable with population growth, poverty, overcrowding, deforestation, cheap air travel and the dangerous treatment of animals for food. We also warned that the NHS microbiology and virology services necessary to provide local surveillance and testing in the event of any disease outbreak have been defunded and fragmented over a decade. Many services have been outsourced to a distant hub with no on-site training or research opportunities for future pathologists. A properly funded service could have stockpiled equipment, reagents and swabs likely to be needed for testing – ideally sourced locally – but instead we have become entirely reliant on Chinese supplies in such an emergency. The risks have been in plain view for a decade. The Royal College of Pathologists should be shouting this from the rooftops."

Bottom line

A SECOND wave of Covid-19 isn't certain. With luck, it will wilt in the heat or some may have T-cell immunity to the virus that doesn't show up on tests. But given only 7 percent of us may have been infected so far, half of those infected spread without any symptoms and only half with symptoms isolate properly, it's a big risk. Add in lockdown easing and school return before Test and Trace is running smoothly, with full beaches, unlimited English travel and the Cummings factor, and it becomes even more likely. So wash your hands again, wear a mask in crowds and keep your distance, particularly from day-trippers with dodgy eyesight.

---

22 May: Quarantine measures announced requiring UK arrivals to self-isolate for 14 days from 8 June. **23 May**: Dominic Cummings, PM's chief political adviser, is revealed to have travelled 260 miles to Durham during lockdown. **28 May**: Contact tracing begins in England and Scotland. **30 May**: Vulnerable people who are shielding can go outside and meet one person from another family while maintaining social distancing. **1 June**: Schools in England begin phased reopening.

MD on Matters of life and death

Private Eye 1524   Press day: 15 June
1,307 daily cases   **84** daily deaths   **39,395** UK deaths to date

Blind to data

THE government isn't alone in making serious errors in the pandemic. Many thousands of people might still be alive today if the scientific advice determining the timing of the lockdown had been more accurate, based on data that was available at the time.

Most of the focus so far has been on the lack of adequate personal protective equipment (PPE), failure to protect care homes and the folly of stopping a test, trace and isolate (TTI) programme in March. The UK did not have a proper plan or capacity, and yet some countries with a comprehensive TTI programme from the start avoided lockdown altogether. People have been able to go about their socially distanced lives sensibly managing their own risk. This has to be our Plan A next time. TTI is essential.

PPE is also essential to protect frontline staff from high viral loads but was in short supply just when it was most needed. And in the mad scramble to save the NHS, many elderly people carrying the virus were discharged to care homes without a test and under the government's instructions. Lots of deaths followed. NHS infection control experts and the Care Quality Commission should have stepped in to stop it.

In the absence of TTI, lockdown in the UK became inevitable and the timing was crucial. Get it right, and you reduce deaths dramatically, come out sooner and minimise harm to the economy, livelihoods, education and those needing treatment for, say, cancer. Get it wrong, and the deaths mount up quickly and we delay coming out. We got the science wrong.

Scientific error

BACK in March, Covid-19 was spreading far more rapidly than the government was being advised. As MD observed: "Most experts outside the government circle worry that the UK is two weeks behind the curve... the evidence from China and Italy was clear that tougher measures would be needed... Johnson has ignored evidence-based advice from the WHO [World Health Organization]" (*Eye* 1519).

A key problem was lack of access to the government's scientific advice. The Scientific Pandemic Influenza Group on Modelling (SPI-M) was reporting to the Scientific Advisory Group for Emergencies (SAGE), but membership, meetings and minutes were secret. These committees reach a consensus view on what to advise, which can of course be wrong. It is more likely to be corrected quickly if it is open to scrutiny.

Not so SAGE advice

THE government's first big press conference on coronavirus was on 12 March. The number of deaths in Italy had risen rapidly to more than 1,000 in a few weeks, and the UK was on notice. Sir Patrick Vallance, chief scientific adviser, announced: "We're maybe four weeks or so behind Italy based on the scale of the outbreak." In fact, we officially reached 1,000 Covid-19 deaths 16 days later. With retrospective data, we now know we hit 1,000 deaths just 12 days after Italy.

This was suspected by many at the time, based purely on deaths in hospitals. Official counts of infection were doubling every three days. And yet the SPI-M modelling advice to SAGE, and hence to government, was that infections were doubling every five to six days. Boris Johnson announced on 16 March: "According to SAGE, without drastic action, cases could double every five to six days." In fact, they had been doubling every three days for the previous two weeks. The government was given and was giving out the wrong advice. Yet it had the data to show it was wrong at the time.

From SPI-M to SAGE

WE now have access to minutes which show that both SPI-M and SAGE agreed that the doubling time was five to seven days in March. However, some of the smaller groups contributing to SPI-M had come up with more accurate doubling times of three days.

Consensus is never easy and the big players in the world of modelling, such as Imperial College under the leadership of Prof Neil Ferguson, tend to win out. The Imperial College model won, using early data out of Wuhan at the start of the pandemic to estimate how many people are likely to be infected by each person (the R number), and how long it takes those people to get infected. Based on this, they advised the government of five to seven days for infections to double.

This Chinese data was always at odds with the more recent UK data, and by recalculating with this and other Italian data available at the time, we get a doubling time of three days by 14 March, and the need for earlier lockdown. Johnson should have announced this on 16 March, not 23 March. He might even have escaped infection and his own near-death experience. If an infection doubles every three days rather than six, then after a month every single infection has spread to 1,024 people rather than 32. That's a huge difference.

Ferguson 'fess up?

HAVING resigned from SAGE for breaking the lockdown rules, but still working as an adviser on SPI-M, Prof Ferguson told the Commons science committee on 10 June that deaths would "at least have been halved" had the UK locked down a week earlier. More than 20,000 people would still be alive today, and probably many of the 200 younger health and social care staff who have died. Ferguson added that policies to protect care homes and the elderly "failed to be enacted". He did not say that data available at the time strongly indicated that his unit's modelling was inaccurate and contributed to late lockdown. [*Note: There were many modelling and data estimates early in the pandemic, when testing wasn't widely available, and numbers have since been revised. The public inquiry should determine whether the right action was taken at the right time.*]

BAME blame

THE government ordered a review of why BAME citizens were at more risk of death from Covid-19, and promptly censored the findings. However, the probable reasons aren't hard to work out. Poverty kills.

BAME citizens are more likely to be in poorly paid employment. These are often insecure, gig economy jobs with no pay if you take time off to self-isolate or self-shield. Work, and risk lives. Or starve. Security guards, taxi drivers and bus drivers have died in disproportionate numbers. The cost of living in an unequal society can be your life.

Of the 200 deaths of NHS and care staff from Covid-19 [*Note: As of June 2021, the figure was 1,500*], 60 percent have been BAME workers.

Many have been doing low paid frontline care, with high exposure to viral loads with no, or inadequate, PPE. Those who try to speak up and raise safety concerns are often marginalised and ignored. Of the whistleblowing stories MD has covered in 28 years, over half come from BAME staff who refuse to be silenced. All sacrificed their jobs, health and livelihoods to speak up.

What next?

THE virus exists merely to replicate. If it kills its host, it dies with it, so my guess is it will eventually evolve into a less virulent form and may join our seasonal offering of flu. However, by this September it could still be pretty lethal for the elderly, so a second wave in the cold weather is a significant risk for them.

The risk to children is remarkably low. If you're aged 5-14 and you haven't had it yet, your chance of death from Covid is 1 in 3,579,551. You are more likely to die walking to school.

As statistician Professor Sir David Spiegelhalter observes: "For women aged 30–34, around 1 in 70,000 died from Covid over the nine peak weeks of the epidemic. Over 80 percent of these had pre-existing medical conditions. So a healthy woman in this age-group had less than a 1 in 350,000 risk of dying from Covid, around 1/4 of the normal risk of an accidental death over this period." However, more than 15,000 people have died in care homes.

Risk revisited

RISK can never be eliminated but it can be managed. Our tolerance of different risks is influenced more by experience than science. If you've spent the last three months treating people fighting for breath with Covid-19, you're unlikely to go on a march or a trip to the beach just yet. If you've been a victim of vile racism but not the virus, you may well decide to march. If you're a child who's more likely to die from a lightning strike than Covid-19, you'll wonder why you're being kept indoors (except during a lightning storm). If you're shielding with cancer and have six months to live, you may say: "Fuck it, I want my friends around me" and reassure them not to feel guilty if they give you the infection. "Come inside my bubble, even if it kills me."

In the absence of a police state, and the presence of ever-changing government guidance, many people are making their own minds up about risk, as they always have done. In a sense, that's what health is. The freedom to live a life that you have reason to value, and the responsibility not to harm others in doing so. Wash your hands, keep your distance, go outside, wear a mask on public transport, avoid mass gatherings, spend some money if you have any left. The UK may be heading for one of the worst "death rate-economic crash-education crash" combos in the world. But we can still be kind.

Viral reminders

YOU ARE safer outdoors. Wind, heat and UV light protect you.

The SARS-CoV-2 virus is fragile. It breaks up simply by using soap and water. Hand washing is a highly effective weapon. Try not to touch your eyes, nose or mouth. The highest-risk environments are enclosed, with a high density of people. The virus travels in droplets of fluid. A single cough produces 3,000 droplets releasing 200m virus particles at 50mph. Heavier droplets fall to the floor or surfaces. Others travel up to 2m, but if you're less than 2m for less than 15 minutes, the risk is low. If in doubt, wear a clean mask and handle it hygienically. Know your numbers. Healthy under 45s are at much less personal risk of harm, even at 1 metre, and school children are at tiny personal risk. The risks to them of not going to school are far greater. Are we prepared to accept slightly more risk ourselves as adults to reduce the widespread harm to children?

---

5 June: WHO encourages more use of face masks. UK makes masks compulsory on public transport from 15 June. **9 June**: UK records lowest daily Covid-19 death toll since 22 March. **13 June**: "Social bubble" scheme announced allowing single-person households to meet and stay overnight with another household. **15 June**: Global cases hit 8m. UK non-essential shops reopen.

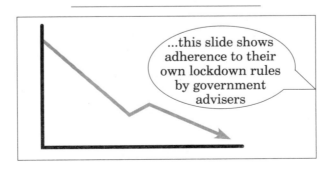

...this slide shows adherence to their own lockdown rules by government advisers

MD on Health for all

Private Eye 1525   **Press day: 29 June**

815 daily cases   **52** daily deaths   **40,341** UK deaths to date

Health for All

THE World Health Organization (WHO) has had a lot on its plate since it promised in 1975 to deliver "Health for All by the Year 2000". The theory was that every citizen would have an acceptable level of health if they had access to primary healthcare. Interventions (vaccination, contraception, oral rehydration, breast feeding, child surveillance, kindness) are relatively cheap, highly effective and can be delivered at or close to home.

"Health for All by 2000" failed; not just because the 134 governments who signed up weren't all fully committed but because HIV/AIDS struck in 1981. Like SARS-CoV-2, it crossed over from animals, and has since infected more than 70m people and 35m people have died. The virus is still with us and we still don't have a vaccine.

Who's listening?

LAST year the WHO declared that global health threat levels were now so high, every government should make 2019 "the year of health emergency preparedness". But was anyone listening?

WHO even named its top 10 global health threats, all of which are inter-connected: 1. Air pollution and climate change; 2. Non-communicable diseases; 3. A global influenza pandemic; 4. Fragile, vulnerable settings; 5. Antimicrobial resistance; 6. Ebola and high threat pathogens; 7. Weak primary care; 8. Vaccine hesitancy; 9. Dengue; and 10. HIV. All remain active threats and will do so if governments only focus on Number 3 and ignore the others.

Good(ish) news

SURPRISINGLY, the mass UK gatherings outside – from VE Day onwards – have yet to be followed by significant spikes in hospital admissions and deaths from Covid-19. They could yet happen, but so far, so lucky.

The prevalence of the virus in the community is currently 0.06 percent, so for every 10,000 people in a crowd, six will likely be infectious. The virus is easily destroyed outdoors, particularly in hot weather. The risks of gatherings are more the cramming into cars or public transport to get there or going inside to use toilets or to seek food. Those present tend to be younger and less at risk of serious infection, although a single infection can spark a mass outbreak if you work or live in a high-risk environment.

In Leicester, there has been a spike of 658 cases in a community with multi-generational households and a sandwich factory. There have been other clusters in UK food processing plants. In Germany, a single infection led to an outbreak of 1,500 workers in a meat processing factory. Workers crammed together at a temperature below 5°C with loud machinery so they have to shout, is ideal for spread.

Quarantining

ORDERING people arriving in the UK to self-isolate for 14 days so late in the pandemic was always fairly pointless and would certainly worsen the economic pain. It would have been far more effective when prevalence was higher. It makes no sense for people arriving from those countries where the prevalence is currently lower than the UK (ie everywhere in continental Europe apart from Sweden). There are only six large countries currently ahead of us in prevalence (Brazil, Mexico, Peru, Sweden, Chile and Saudi Arabia) with the US just behind us. It would make more sense for every other country to quarantine us on the way in.

The UK may now be lifting quarantine for many countries in return for reciprocal freedoms, but airports and planes remain ideal spreading grounds for the six in 10,000 passengers infected. MD won't be holidaying abroad any time soon.

Educational gap

IN 60 percent of private primary schools and 85 percent of private secondary schools, pupils have been receiving a full timetable of live video lessons during lockdown, starring their subject teachers across the whole curriculum. In state schools the corresponding figures are 5 percent and 11 percent.

Private pupils are also more likely to have a quiet space to work in, a laptop to work on and high-speed broadband. Eighty percent of state schools are offering an online platform of work, and if work is submitted for marking, state and private teachers score equally in their percentage and speed of marking. However, state school pupils – particularly in poorer areas – have been much less likely to submit work for marking. In state schools that have opened, two-thirds of pupils have attended in wealthy areas but under half in the poorest areas. Left behind children are being left further behind.

Tests before tracing

THE government has pledged to increase testing to more than 200,000 tests every day, but has not always succeeded. On 19 June, however, it boasted that more than 230,000 tests had been done. But 74,000 of these were antibody tests that try to detect people long after they've been infected. Subtract the tests done for research and the tests sent in the post that haven't yet been returned, and just 74,000 PCR (polymerase chain reaction) swab tests were done for diagnostic purposes. And for the last month the government has refused to say whether the 74,000 tests were on 74,000 different people or if many people had more than one test.

Partial Test and Trace

BETWEEN 25 May and 7 June, a large Office for National Statistics (ONS) representative sample calculated the community prevalence of SARS-CoV-2 infection to be 0.06 percent. So for England, NHS Test

"I said you're standing too close!"

and Trace had 33,000 customers to find, to trace their close contacts and to persuade them to get tested and isolate. Yet just 12,600 positive lab tests in England were referred to NHS Test and Trace in that week, and more than 4,000 were double counted tests. So there were just 8,117 people to follow up and trace, leaving around 25,000 roaming free. A fully functioning Test and Trace phone app may have improved contact tracing and reduced viral spread, but this formerly "essential service" has been abandoned by health secretary Matt Hancock at a loss of £11.8m. All of which makes a second wave more likely.

Antibody testing

ANTIBODY tests are Hancock's latest toy, and he's bought millions. They aim to tell you if you've been infected or not, but they can't prove you're immune to reinfection. It's a massive money-making venture – they're easy and cheap to produce, with little quality control or market regulation – and there are more than 200 on the market, some claiming an impossible "100 percent accuracy".

If you're going to make detectable levels of antibodies after infection (not everyone will), it takes at least 14 days and often longer. Roche (one company the government has bought from), claims 100 percent accuracy on the basis of a subgroup of eight people who, 40 days after they were known to be infected from a PCR swab test, all tested positive for antibodies.

However, the subgroup was cherry-picked from a sample of 93 patients known to have had Covid-19, of which 15 (16 percent) tested negative for antibodies. So hardly 100 percent. The danger of this PR sales tactic of data dredging, slicing and spin is that it discredits science at a time when vaccine compliance may be the only thing that defeats the virus. The more tricks the drug company marketeers use, the less their products will be trusted – another gift for the anti-vaccination movement.

Old people die anyway

ON 11 June, the *Daily Telegraph* published an interview with cancer specialist Karol Sikora, aka the Positive Professor, who stated that the "Covid-19 death toll may be less than half of what has been recorded because many victims of the pandemic would have died soon anyway".

A wider debate is raging about those dying "with" or "of" Covid-19. Some argue those with chronic conditions (dementia, diabetes, heart failure, frailty of old age) die from those conditions brought forward a few months by Covid-19; others argue that they might still be alive for a long time without Covid-19. Who is right?

The highest death toll has been in care homes, and the average length of stay in a single residential care home in England that ended in death is around 26 months (not counting previous stays in other homes.) So residents who die from Covid-19 – even if they have other chronic illnesses as nearly all of them do – may be having their lives cut short by up to 26 months.

The current high excess deaths may be followed by a subsequent reduction in expected deaths, as commonly happens after heatwaves and flu seasons, but it is impossible to say if or when this will happen.

Although the average life expectancy in the UK is currently 81.25 years, if you actually make it to your 80th birthday, your life expectancy is nine years for a man and 10 years for a woman. Even an 80-year-old obese male smoker has a life expectancy of five years outside of a care home. So although Covid-19 predominantly kills the sick and elderly, many would have lived for months or even years without it. Some residents may have welcomed a Covid death when it came, but if we'd locked down a week earlier and protected care homes properly, many thousands of people would still be alive. The end of year excess death figures will tell us how many may have died in the next six months.

Recovery position

TWO weeks ago, RECOVERY trial researchers in Oxford announced "a major breakthrough" in the battle against Covid-19 that was "globally applicable". Cheap-as-chips dexamethasone "reduced the 28-day mortality rate of Covid-19 by 17 percent, with a highly significant trend showing the greatest benefit among patients needing ventilation."

This sounded like great news, but the results were announced at a press conference which didn't back its claims with a published, peer reviewed paper or a preprint. This is bad science, buckling under the pressure to get some good news out there before it's been independently scrutinised. Please don't do this with vaccines.

The preliminary report has now been released and the benefits are quite selective. If you treat eight seriously ill Covid-19 patients on oxygen and mechanical ventilation with dexamethasone, you save one life. For those on oxygen only, you need to treat 25 patients to save one life. If you have Covid-19 but don't need oxygen or ventilation, dexamethasone is more likely to cause harm than good.

Generally, the more critically ill patients are, the more they benefit from treatment. But in this case, the vast majority of people who die from Covid-19 are over 70, and of these very few are deemed fit enough for ventilation and only 6 percent are put on oxygen. So dexamethasone is a big breakthrough for younger patients (most people on mechanical ventilators are in their 50s and 60s; 40 percent currently die), but it won't make any difference to the elderly or shift the overall death rate much.

---

19 June: UK Covid-19 alert lowered from level 4 to 3 (substantial risk, general circulation). Revised figures show death count exceeded 1,000 for 22 consecutive days in the spring. **23 June**: PM announces relaxation of restrictions and 2m social distancing rule. **24 June**: Volunteers receive injections of a vaccine developed by Oxford University. UK health officials warn of the risk of a second wave. **26 June**: Government changes quarantine rules to allow people to holiday in Spain, Greece and elsewhere from 6 July. **29 June**: Matt Hancock announces first local lockdown, in Leicester, from 4 July.

MD on The road to recovery

Private Eye 1526   Press day: 13 July
584 daily cases   **23** daily deaths   **40,855** UK deaths to date

The recovery position

A KEY ingredient of health is our ability to recover when shit happens. Everyone must learn to live with loss eventually – a loved one, a livelihood, a liberty or a bodily function – but in global emergencies the losses come thick and fast, causing a second wave of fear and anxiety.

The death toll from Covid-19 would be far higher had countries not tried to prevent viral spread; but the economic, educational and health consequences of lockdown are likely to cast a long shadow, particularly for those who were neck high in shit to start with. So what are the best routes to recovery?

Share the data

COVID-19 reminds us that we live with risk every day. The risks posed by this particular threat are determined by the competence of our political and public health leaders, how generously we fund our health and care services, our individual and collective behaviour and the evolution of the virus. There is still much we don't know (like how much viral spread is airborne).

In trying to defeat one risk, we mustn't neglect others. We modelled the risks of the virus but not the risks of social isolation, lost education, delayed diagnoses and worsening inequality. Following the science means embracing uncertainty, publishing all models and data for public scrutiny, inviting challenge, admitting error, changing direction when needed and treating the public as informed participants. If our controlling government and its advisers had shared data earlier, we might have locked down a week earlier and halved the death toll. It took four days to turn around test results in the Leicester outbreak, and 11 days for Public Health England to communicate the results to local councils. Local directors of public health must be in charge of local test and trace, so they can respond to outbreaks immediately.

Understand evolution

THE SARS-CoV-2 virus may have originated fairly recently in live animal markets, or it may have been hiding out in bat caves for years, waiting for the right moment. But in over-crowding and over-consuming, humans have created environments that allow ever-adaptable microbes to kill us.

Deforestation, burning fossil fuels, polluting water, dumping waste, mistreating animals, overusing drugs, tolerating extreme poverty and ignoring large scale displacement – all have created a perfect storm for harmful microbe evolution and uninhabitable weather (2020 started not with Covid-19, but horrific bush fires).

We may, or may not, develop a vaccine to save us from Covid-19, but we definitely need to reduce the risk of further health emergencies. Health and wellbeing of people and planet must now be the paramount political concern. Economic growth must not happen at the expense of global health.

Global health

WITH around 550,000 global deaths so far, the Covid-19 pandemic barely registers in the all-time "shit happens" league table. Far more avoidable deaths occur every year, and at far younger age, due to global warming, dirty air and water, endemic diseases such as TB, malaria, HIV and dengue, junk food, alcohol, smoking, prescription drugs, recreational drugs, antibiotic resistance, war, famine, economic displacement, lack of access to healthcare and vaccine refusal.

Unlike Covid-19, these deaths don't suddenly tank rich economies, so they are largely ignored. But they are all interlinked. It will need concerted global collaboration to move towards "health for all", not a retreat into self-protective nationalism.

National Sickness Service

IN its 72 years, the NHS has been far more a sickness service than a health service. GP and community services are hugely over-burdened, public health services have been cut to the bone and we've become much less effective than we could be at preventing illness, as Covid-19 has shown. Half the deaths would have been avoided had we been on to it more quickly.

Much of the cancer, heart disease, cerebrovascular disease, diabetes, liver failure, kidney failure and suicide that currently kills people well before their time could also be prevented. But it would require government to accept that health is more socially, environmentally and economically determined than, say, how many press-ups a prime minister can do for a photo op in the *Mail on Sunday* after a lifetime of privilege.

It is also true the health of people working in the NHS and in care services was poor before the pandemic. If we do not want to face a haemorrhaging of staff from stress and exhaustion, they must be supported and helped to recover too. And help will be needed for those recovering from hospitalisation and intensive care, and those still grieving for friends and relatives who died in isolation. How we die matters as much as when we die.

Ration the regulations

IN England, the Care Quality Commission costs £234m annually (2018-19), the cost of a district general hospital every year. It costs the NHS the same again because of the time taken to manage inspections.

Trusts and GP practices spend months preparing for and managing CQC inspections, when their time, energy and money would be far better spent serving patients, particularly now NHS waiting times are so high. What the NHS and care system needs is

Last Orders

a slimmed down independent safety inspectorate, solely focused on analysing safety data and responding to serious concerns raised by staff, patients and carers – and supporting and protecting them to do so. Such a system could have stopped the horrors of rogue surgeon Ian Paterson and the harms of vaginal mesh, which the current crop of bloated and self-protective regulators singularly failed to do (read the excellent Cumberlege Review).

Out with outsourcing...

AN EVEN greater sum of NHS money is wasted on the hugely complex bureaucracy needed to support an entirely unnecessary market system obsessed with outsourcing. Very rarely has outsourcing improved the quality, safety or value of services, with Test and Trace the most recent £10bn fiasco.

Boris Johnson is busy outsourcing blame to care homes, claiming there would have been far fewer deaths if more had "followed procedures" when untested patients were transferred from the NHS. But care homes did not have adequate PPE or testing kits. Those that did well were generally small, family run units with permanent staff on a shoestring budget. Large chains, such as HC-One Care Homes, lost 863 residents and three staff to Covid. Their operating company, HC-One Ltd, made a £6.5m loss in 2018, yet paid out £40m in rent to

offshore firms and pays its chief executive £800,000 a year. It employs a lot of insecure agency staff, who move around homes.

We need a *united* not-for-profit health and social care system where staff are valued and everyone is treated according to need, not ability to pay, and savings are reinvested in services. We need regional public health boards led by experts from the communities they serve. And we need to make public health a priority, not just for disease outbreaks but for the ever-present emergencies of climate change, air pollution, poverty, inequality, obesity, smoking, substance abuse, mental illness, antibiotic resistance and vaccine hesitancy. If a second wave of Covid comes, we need to be as fit as we can to withstand it.

Vaccines for all?

A VACCINE may yet allow people to live, work, travel, learn and socialise together safely again, but it must not be an excuse to carry on as before.

The first big test of the global concordance in health is not whether safe and effective vaccines for SARS-CoV-2 can be produced in record time (95 percent of vaccine attempts fail, and the previous fastest turn-around was four years, for mumps), but whether they will be shared affordably and fairly. The second test will be whether enough people want to take them to achieve herd immunity, given the poisonous and profitable growth of the anti-vaxx industry (see the excellent report by the Centre for Countering Digital Hate).

State of play

THERE are currently around 200 candidates in "preclinical evaluation" for a SARS-CoV-2 vaccine, and 16 in clinical trials. Who gets there first (China, America, UK, Germany, South Africa or India) may determine who gets the vaccine first. The idea of the whole world coming together to roll out a single vaccine for everyone is a pipe dream.

America has just bought more than 500,000 doses of the anti-viral drug remdesivir – the entire global production in July and 90 percent of August and September's production. It appears to reduce the time patients spend in hospital but there is no evidence yet that it saves lives. If an American or Chinese company comes up with a vaccine that works, it is likely to stay in the home country first. Vaccine nationalism could get ugly.

Oxford union

THE team at Oxford University's Jenner Institute is using a "viral vector". This is a weakened common cold adenovirus that infects chimpanzees, that is then tweaked for humans and has the genetic material to build SARS-CoV-2 spike glycoproteins inserted into it. This in turn should trigger an immune response. The Oxford team is starting phase three human trials. However, the prevalence of SARS-CoV-2 infection in the UK is now so low (good news, unless you're in research) that trials are being extended to Brazil, South Africa, the US and elsewhere. The collaboration with AstraZeneca has US and UK funding and is also looking for volunteers (*https://covid19vaccinetrial.co.uk/participate-trial*).

Children first?

ONE side effect of lockdown is that many parents have been reluctant to leave home and children have missed vaccinations to protect them for infections likely to cause them far more harm than Covid-19.

Even before the pandemic, the US was facing its highest measles tally in 27 years, with 31 states having nearly 1,300 cases in 2019. There have been widespread outbreaks across Europe too. In England, the number of MMR vaccines delivered dropped by 20 percent in the first three weeks of lockdown, and smaller falls were reported in infant vaccines in Scotland. We are making a huge global effort to find a vaccine for a disease that barely harms children but not nearly enough effort to provide them with the vaccines we know help prevent deadly diseases. The last thing a world fighting Covid needs are global outbreaks of measles, whooping cough and diphtheria.

Post-viral fatigue

THE TOLL of post-Covid fatigue is likely to be significant and there are currently no drugs to magic it away, although research is under way and there are coping strategies.

The basic ingredients of health are well-known, well-evidenced and fairly easily remembered using the mnemonic CLANGERS, as in: Connect; Learn; (be) Active; Notice; Give back; Eat well; Relax; Sleep.

Friendship and a feeling of belonging; an ability and curiosity to learn and adapt; purposeful physical and mental activity; observation and appreciation of the environment; compassion for others; food that is both delicious and nutritious; an ability to switch off and relax and regular, restorative sleep – collectively these daily joys of health are more powerful than any drug.

The privileged can do them every day, even in lockdown. If we all managed them, we would barely need the NHS. But if you're living with debt, discrimination, depression, domestic abuse, drug addiction, dementia, etc, they are much harder to achieve. The focus on prevention, helping others and lifestyle medicine is a lot cheaper and more enjoyable than medicating for diabetes and depression. Indeed, it's the one thing that can keep communities alive and health services viable. MD – who works in the field – has produced a short film on coping with post-viral fatigue and how to get your five portions of fun a day (*www.youtube. com/watch?v=bbdlMWXiHoc*).

---

4 July: UK pubs, restaurants, barbers and places of worship reopen on "Super Saturday". **7 July:** Three England pubs close after positive coronavirus tests. **8 July:** Government unveils £30bn plan to prevent mass unemployment, including giving businesses a £1,000 bonus for every staff member kept on. Fifty percent discounts introduced for public to eat out in August. **10 July:** UK rejects offer to join EU vaccine programme. **13 July:** Face masks to be compulsory in shops in England from 24 July (having been compulsory in Scotland since 10 July).

"It's to replace the Test and Trace app"

MD on The new abnormal

Private Eye 1527   Press day: 27 July
736 daily cases   **16** daily deaths   **41,114** UK deaths to date

The cover-up

YOU would think, 17 years on from SARS 2003 and after multiple pandemic warnings since then, that definitive research would have proven the case for masks in public, and what type of masks to wear. It hasn't. If masks do work, they are more likely to reduce infection during the heat of an outbreak, rather than at the tail end of it.

Masks are being introduced on the back of observational studies, rather than definitive randomised controlled trials (RCTs). Just as we don't have "RCT proof" that eye protection, social distancing, quarantining or coughing into your elbow work, so it is with masks. Britain is leading the world in drug and vaccine trials for Covid. Now we need large-scale trials of masks and SARS-CoV-2 spread.

Logic failure

MASKS – if properly used – may reduce (but not stop) viral shedding by people who don't realise they are infected. (Those with symptoms should be isolating indoors, not using masks as an excuse to go out.) How widely adopted they will be in the various nations of the UK remains to be seen.

To avoid confusion, many countries use the simplest advice – to always wear a mask in public. In England, you now need to carry an entirely illogical checklist to remind you when you do and don't have to mask up. Masks are obligatory in shops, enclosed shopping centres, banks, building societies, post offices, railway and bus stations, airports, on public transport and when queuing for food. They are voluntary in pubs and restaurants, libraries, museums, galleries, solicitors' and accountants' offices, cinemas, theatres, concert and bingo halls, conference centres, casinos, gyms, leisure centres, spas, beauty salons, auction houses and when walking around your house when you know you're infected.

Masks do not reduce your oxygen saturation but they can only work if used correctly, and yet many spectacle-wearers steam up and lower the mask below the nose, which is akin to wearing underpants with your penis on the outside. Repeatedly touching your mask (or penis) is poor infection control, as is leaving it lying around on the sideboard after use. Disposable masks are a pollution hazard and unaffordable for some, who may also struggle to regularly wash and dry cloth masks. Reused disposable masks and unwashed cloth masks comply with the law but may spread the virus. Will there be mask banks for the poor? Will you need a mask to enter them?

National differences

HAS Scotland managed the pandemic better than England? Both Scottish and English residents seem to think so, but beating England in pandemic management is an open goal.

When Nicola Sturgeon was asked to defend Scotland's poor showing on excess mortality (30 times the rate of Norway), she said: "The figures are still much higher than we want them to be, but they are lower than the excess deaths in England." In excess deaths per million people, England has around 970, Scotland 860, Wales 700 and Northern Ireland 500. Within countries, outbreaks are concentrated in poorer, crowded areas, and England has more of those (in London, the North-east, the North-west and the Midlands).

Scotland made many of the mistakes England did. It didn't control its borders; it was poorly prepared with PPE and failed to protect care homes; it didn't have the capacity to test and trace. Its first outbreak was at a Nike conference at the Hilton Carlton Hotel in Edinburgh on 26-27 February, attended by more than 70 employees from all over the world. At least 25 people linked to the event were confirmed to have been infected – eight resident in Scotland. Health authorities in Scotland were aware of the outbreak by 2 March, but the public were not told about it. Epidemiologists at the University of Edinburgh estimate that half the Scottish Covid deaths would have been prevented by earlier lockdown. And the chief medical officer resigned after breaking her own lockdown rules. So far, so English.

England first

THE main reason England has seen higher excess death rates is that the pandemic hit England – particularly London – first. All four home countries were behind the infection curve when they locked down on 23 March, but England was most behind.

In the days of hunter-gatherers, it could take 10,000 years for an infection that required close physical contact to spread from, say, China to London. Now it can happen in hours thanks to aeroplanes. Island nations stand the best chance of controlling infections if they control their borders, as New Zealand, Australia, Iceland and the "virtual island" of South Korea have shown. The UK decided against strict border control.

From 1 January to the day of lockdown in the UK, 16m people flew into UK airports and only 273 were quarantined. Even after the WHO declared a global emergency on 30 January, we welcomed passengers from Covid hotspots (90,000 from Milan in February alone, and 20,000 a day from Spain). Most of the travel was to English airports, particularly in London, hence the pandemic seeded there first. In February and early March, all passengers from Hubei province in China and certain areas of South Korea, as well as Iran and later Italy, were asked to self-isolate for 14 days on arrival (but not Spain for some reason). But this was entirely voluntary and widely flouted.

Zero Covid

THE Scottish policy only diverged markedly from England's after 10 May, when Boris Johnson announced his "roadmap to reopen society" by encouraging people to "stay alert". It was met with derision by Sturgeon. Scotland is instead pursuing a path of elimination, or so-called "zero Covid". It's a bold promise, built on a more effective test and trace system than England's, longer lockdown, earlier compulsory masks and three more weeks of pub closures.

Out of order

ZERO Covid is a much easier target for the public to understand and support than, say, "orderly infection", but Prof Chris Whitty, England's chief medical officer and SAGE member, doesn't think it's likely. As he admitted in the Downing Street press conference on 23 June: "I would be surprised and delighted if we weren't in this current situation through the winter and into next spring. I think then let's regroup and work out where we are. But I expect there to be a significant amount of coronavirus circulating at least until that time."

Meanwhile, Independent SAGE, a group of public health experts with no government ties, believes zero Covid across the UK is desirable and achievable. The theory is that more economic and social pain now would lead to fewer deaths and a faster return to complete normality. It would require stricter border controls, improvements to test and trace and a reintroduction of more stringent measures of social control until the outbreak is under a weekly average of one new case per million per day. It would also require a highly unlikely U-turn from Johnson, although he has hastily imposed a Spanish quarantine.

Testing times

THE prevalence of coronavirus is now low, even in England, so there is no excuse for local outbreaks not to be dealt with quickly. Nobody gives a fig how many tests a day the government claims to be doing. What matters is that the right people are tested in the right places at the right time, to shut down local outbreaks, prevent deaths, avoid a large second wave and another national lockdown. This requires local public health experts *and GPs* to have the data, resources and power to manage outbreaks quickly.

There is also no excuse for not regularly testing NHS and care staff. The government's target of keeping deaths below 20,000 was undone not just by late lockdown, but also by denying tests to frontline staff, many of whom were working, changing and meeting in cramped surroundings and passing the virus between themselves. Health and care workers were six times more likely to be carrying the virus, hence the high incidence of spread in hospitals and care homes. Far too many patients, residents and staff died for want of a functional test, trace and isolate programme when it was most needed.

Only following orders

FRONTLINE staff were crying out to be protected with PPE and tested for infection in March; yet as we locked down, this directive was circulating in London hospitals: "There is currently a critical shortage of the reagent used in Covid-19 testing. In common with other trusts in London, we could run out of tests in a matter of days if the current rate of testing continues. It is essential we reserve Covid-19 tests for patients who

need them most. Currently, the only people who should be tested are:
1. Patients with suspected Covid-19 who are being admitted to hospital.
2. Those already in hospital who develop new symptoms compatible with
Covid-19. Please remember that there are no circumstances in which
people who don't meet this criteria [sic] should be tested: this currently
includes staff." (It also included patients discharged to care homes.)

Long-term prospects

THE eradication of smallpox and imminent eradication of polio
required safe and effective vaccines, and the same is likely to be true for
Covid-19. It could mutate into a more or less virulent form, but currently
it's behaving like a sexually transmitted infection. Many people are
passing it on before they realise they have it. The death rate is strongly
age-related and if you're under 35, you're more likely to die this year in
a road traffic accident.

The long-term effects of infection can be very unpleasant, so it's still
best avoided. When the flu season arrives, it will be impossible initially
for staff to distinguish between Covid and flu, and some people may get
both, so the plan is to get at least half the population vaccinated against
flu, although – as with any Covid vaccines – there will be unfair global
competition for supplies.

Treatment delays

A BIGGER current challenge for the NHS is to tackle the waiting list
backlog. However, many patients are refusing treatment because of
the requirement to self-isolate for 14 days prior to admission. Many
would require financial support to cover loss of earnings, and help with
accommodation too. Currently, they are not allowed to share a bed or
bathroom with anyone.

As self-isolation is a mandatory part of their treatment, this period
should be included in statutory sick pay. The NHS is facing many last-
minute cancellations which they can't fill because of the two-week
isolation requirement.

Reasons to be cheerful

MD did not see the pandemic coming and we will never know the true
number of Covid deaths in the UK. We will have missed thousands at

the beginning because of lack of testing, and we have added some in England where anyone who ever tested positive is currently counted as a Covid death (even if they die much later of something else). What we can say (again) is that 999 out of 1,000 of us *haven't* died from Covid-19. And, as MD predicted, there has been a lull after the storm, with excess deaths in England and Wales now below the five-year average for the fourth consecutive week.

Our new passion for handwashing and social distancing has – as predicted – reduced the incidence of flu, colds, viral hepatitis, asthma, tonsillitis, bronchitis, laryngitis, conjunctivitis, chicken pox and diarrhoeal diseases. There is still an urgent need to improve public health, not just to reduce the risk of dying from Covid, but from greater risks that cause far more premature deaths in the UK every year, from smoking to air pollution. The government is now at least toying with tackling obesity.

There will be local outbreaks in the UK, and more of them in England. But the government's "protective ring" around care homes, hospitals, frontline staff, and those most at risk should finally be a lot less leaky. Success relies on repeatedly testing those at highest risk of spreading or dying, even if they don't have symptoms. If we had done this in March, we may have had localised outbreaks, shielded the vulnerable and reduced deaths without locking down the whole country. But we had neither the tests nor the system. As MD observed in March, you can't beat a virus if you don't know where it is. No excuses next time…

---

15 July: PM commits to "independent inquiry" into pandemic but "now is not the right time". **17 July**: PM announces more easing of restrictions for England, aiming for "significant return to normality" by Christmas. **20 July**: A vaccine from the University of Oxford is found to provide immunity. UK deal for 90m doses of vaccines being developed by BioNtech-Pfizer and Valneva, as well as 100m doses from Oxford-AstraZeneca. **25 July**: Government advises against non-essential travel to Spain and imposes 14-day self-isolation for those returning.

MD on The sick man of Europe

Private Eye 1528   **Press day: 10 August**
960 daily cases   **13** daily deaths   **41,296** UK deaths to date

Going local

NOW that Covid deaths have reduced to a trickle, and excess deaths have been below the five-year average for six weeks, the temptation for those blissfully unaffected is to dismiss the pandemic as a bad dream and our response to it as an absurd overreaction.

Alternatively, the media jumps on every fresh outbreak as evidence of an impending second wave that could be worse than the first. MD takes a middle view. Covid is clearly a deeply unpleasant infectious disease, with both a significant fatality rate and severe long-term health consequences. Doing nothing was never an option.

However, outsourcing was predictably the wrong option. Health secretary Matt Hancock's mates have failed to deliver on test and trace, and trust in the UK government to handle the situation competently has taken a hammering since chief adviser Dominic Cummings' lockdown road trip. The best hope of avoiding another lockdown is for local public health teams and councils to use their local knowledge and expertise when clusters emerge, as many are already doing. Find, test, trace, isolate and support. In Toxteth, a small outbreak was managed by imposing restrictions on just a few streets, with volunteers going door to door to explain them. Such swift local response should avoid the need to shut down a whole city or region.

Who we test

TESTS are most useful and accurate when used in a population most likely to have what you're testing for. Care homes have borne the brunt of Covid deaths and the government wisely promised regular testing of almost 2m residents and staff starting on 6 July.

It now appears to have delayed or abandoned this pledge, which makes no sense, preferring to concentrate on widespread testing of asymptomatic people in the community, where prevalence rates are much lower and the risk of false results is higher. Again, local authorities need to take control of testing where it's needed.

Long Covid

COVID is much less likely to be fatal in the under-50s, but evidence is emerging that it may cause severe long-term health consequences even if the initial infection appeared relatively mild.

A small study of 100 German patients who had recovered from Covid used MRI scans of the heart and found that 78 had "cardiac involvement" and 60 had ongoing myocardial inflammation, which was independent of any other conditions they had, how severe the illness was and how long it lasted (see the journal JAMA Cardiology). Whether this translates to long-term damage remains to be seen. In terms of lung damage, the NHS is anticipating Covid survivors will have more chronic coughs, fibrotic lung disease, bronchiectasis and pulmonary vascular disease.

Those who have been in intensive care will have long-term rehabilitation needs and the Long Covid Support Group is capturing a multitude of symptoms beyond fatigue (*www.longcovid.org*). The Zoe study estimates that up to 10 percent of people with the virus take at least three weeks to recover, with 250,000 people in the UK alone thought to experience symptoms for 30 days or more. Brain fog, chronic pain, headaches, dizziness, nausea, palpitations, shortness of breath, post-exertional malaise and a severe reduction in everyday activities. And many suffer anxiety and low mood. Overall, it's a virus best avoided.

"Do you need to borrow my bikini wax?"

And the winners are...

THE Office for National Statistics (ONS) has published a handy half-way table of deaths, with the most accurate like-for-like comparison of how 23 European countries and regions have fared from January to June 2020. It used two measures: all-cause "excess" mortality compared with the average of the previous five years, and age-standardised mortality rates, which provide a fairer comparison between populations of different sizes and age distributions, rather than a simple count of deaths.

As expected, England came out on top, with nearly 8 percent extra deaths over the five-year average so far, and outbreaks widely spread across the country rather than localised in one or two regions. Spain came in second (7 percent extra), Scotland in third (5 percent) and Belgium in fourth (4 percent). Wales and Northern Ireland are fifth and eighth respectively. Sweden is sixth. Overall, the UK is poorly placed but Scotland has done 60 percent better than England so far, with Wales and Northern Ireland better still. In 14 of the 23 countries considered, age-standardised mortality for 2020 has been below the 2015-19 average. For a nation as wealthy as the UK, we should – and could – have performed better.

How we doctor

HEALTH secretary Matt Hancock is keen to solve the NHS staffing crisis by switching everyone to triage and video consultations before they can see a GP face to face or attend an emergency department. On the plus side, many problems can be safely sorted over phone or video. But complex problems can't be addressed, and serious illness can be easily missed and misdiagnosed without examination.

As any surgeon will tell you: "If you don't put your finger in it, you'll put your foot in it." Also, it's hard to support a grieving elderly patient who isn't tech savvy and has a poor internet connection and a fraction of her face in view. Post-Covid, we may move into the world of disclaimers: we can offer you a video consultation but not a certain diagnosis – and please don't show us your genitals; we can offer you a dental appointment but please sign here that you accept the Covid risk; we can offer you a Covid vaccine or drug but it has been developed much more quickly than we'd like so please sign here to accept any unforeseen side-effects. Proper doctoring and proper science require time, but a pandemic doesn't give you time. So you have to guess, and guess again...

---

30 July: UK increases self-isolation for those testing positive or showing symptoms from seven days to at least ten. Local lockdowns imposed in the North of England. **31 July:** Rising case numbers force PM to postpone some lockdown-easing. **1 August:** Health experts say UK may need to choose between keeping pubs or schools open to limit infection rates. **3 Aug:** "Eat Out to Help Out" scheme begins. **5 Aug:** Commons home affairs committee says spread of virus in UK could have been slowed with earlier quarantine restrictions on arrivals. **6 Aug:** 50m masks bought by government will not be used due to safety concerns. **9 Aug:** Daily confirmed new cases tops 1,000 for the first time since June.

MD on The public health merry-go-round

Private Eye 1529　　**Press day: 24 August**

1,155 daily cases　　**11** daily deaths　　**41,433** UK deaths to date

Loadsamoney...

PREVENTION is not just better than cure, it's usually a lot cheaper too.

The SARS coronavirus outbreak in 2003 cost the global economy $40bn and was contained before it became a pandemic. SARS-CoV-2 is projected to cost up to $8.8 *trillion* by the Asian Development Bank, depending how long it takes for containment. The countries taking the smallest financial hit are those best prepared, with well-funded, fully integrated public health services that were on high alert and ready to go. And then there was England...

Convenient scapegoat

PUBLIC Health England (PHE) is a convenient scapegoat for England's poor pandemic preparedness and response, but to axe it is an admission that the Conservatives' Health and Social Care Act 2012 was a public health disaster.

The government can't say it wasn't warned. From 2011 onwards, when the then health secretary Andrew Lansley announced public health services would transfer from the NHS to local authorities, with many outsourced, senior public health officials have repeatedly warned that fragmentation would lead to massive confusion about who was responsible and accountable for what. The confusion wasn't helped by the creation of PHE, which sits outside the NHS under direct control of the health secretary. Its website is hosted by government and it talks a good game. "Our first duty is to keep people safe... with the capability to respond to public health emergencies round the clock, 365 days a year." If only...

The NHS response is critical in any public health disaster, but having PHE some distance from the action, strategic health authorities and regional public health offices abolished and cash-starved local councils providing frontline services was never going to work in a pandemic.

Professor Hilary Pickles, who spent 14 years at the Department of Health as well as in regional public health, warned the Commons health select committee in 2011: "When the next pandemic strikes, expect public health systems to be in disarray." Now that the next pandemic has struck and public health systems are indeed in disarray, it takes a peculiarly brass neck to pin it on the quango you invented.

Hancock and Hunt off the hook?

MATT HANCOCK is the secretary of state for public health, the NHS and social care. It's far too great a role for a single person, as he is amply proving; but PHE reports to him and if it has failed badly, so has he.

Indeed, when Lansley envisioned PHE, he wanted the day-to-day scandals of the NHS to be outsourced to an NHS commissioning board (now NHS England), leaving him "with a clear line of sight" over public health. The one person with the greatest responsibility for preparing England for a pandemic was Lansley's successor, Jeremy Hunt, followed by Hancock. Neither seems terribly keen to acknowledge this.

Writing on the wall

HUNT, England's longest serving health secretary, knew how poorly prepared the UK was to cope with a pandemic, having overseen the disastrous dry run – Exercise Cygnus – in 2016 (see *Eye* 1521). He clearly hoped it wouldn't happen on his watch.

Last October, with Hancock as health secretary, responsibility for overseeing NHS screening programmes was taken away from PHE and handed to NHS England (along with £600m) after prominent failures and rows about who was accountable and responsible for them. An investigation concluded that the way accountability was structured "creates confusion, delays and risks to patient safety". It could have been written for Covid.

PHE chief executive Duncan Selbie is now rapidly downplaying his organisation's emergency role, ahead of a public inquiry. "The UK had no national diagnostic testing capabilities other than in the NHS at the outset of the pandemic," Selbie said last week. "PHE does not do mass diagnostic testing. We operate national reference and research laboratories focused on novel and dangerous pathogens, and it was never at any stage our role to set the national testing strategy for the coronavirus pandemic. This responsibility rested with the Department of Health and Social Care."

It seems extraordinary that, in seven years of pandemic planning, PHE and the DHSC had not agreed who would be in charge of delivering mass testing. All we can say for sure is that Hunt and Hancock were in charge of both departments and failed to keep people safe.

Public health in England

AFTER 10 years of austerity and seven years of the Health and Social Care Act, England's public health is in predictably bad shape. PHE has seen a budget cut of 15 percent since 2015, and local public health services have been cut by 22 percent. Life expectancy improvements have tailed off. Millions of citizens suffer preventable disease and disability every year, and thousands die young. It starts young too – the UK's paediatric health is scandalously bad.

Poor public health is a prime reason the UK has suffered so many excess deaths during the pandemic. The virus was more deadly for those with chronic disease and the "protect the NHS" message was deadly for those too frightened to seek help for both Covid and non-Covid emergencies. Our recovery plan needs to focus on improving health education and reducing health inequalities. With PHE to be disbanded, it is not yet clear who will take over.

Cock to Koch

HANCOCK's public health focus is on preventing a second wave of Covid, rather than dealing with other public health threats that kill far more of us. His "all new" National Institute for Health Protection (NIHP) sounds suspiciously like the Health Protection Agency, which was reorganised to become part of PHE. [*Note: Since renamed the UK Health Security Agency (UKHSA)*].

Hancock claims NIHP is modelled on the Robert Koch Institute (RKI) in Germany. But there are crucial differences. The RKI has been going for 125 years and reflects the continuity, independence, organisational memory and continuous improvement that stability brings. It is closely aligned with 370 local public health offices, which allow a rapid, coordinated response to health emergencies.

By contrast, NHS regional public health offices were abolished when PHE was created, and it has lasted seven years. It makes some sense to merge PHE's infection control expertise with NHS Test and Trace and the work of the Joint Biosecurity Centre. But NHS Test and Trace has been another multi-billion-pound outsourced disaster, born out of panic when PHE couldn't respond. The money needs to be spent on equipping local public health services, not feathering the nests of private providers and management consultants. Alarmingly, no press were present at Hancock's NIHP launch, but plenty of salivating private stakeholders were.

Think FETTISH

CONTAINMENT of any public health threat depends on effective local systems whose staff have knowledge of communities, schools, workplaces, healthcare systems, networks and cultures. Outsourcing and centralising NHS Test and Trace was the wrong strategy, but not surprising given its boss (Dido Harding) has no public health expertise.

As MD has said repeatedly, infection control requires far more than just "test and trace". It needs accurate data disseminated locally and immediately. Then, think FETTISH – Find, Explain, Test, Trace, Isolate, Support, Home visit (if needed). If you're going to ask those who are already poor, vulnerable and isolated to lock themselves away for 14 days, they need financial and emotional support, and often someone checking their home to make sure they aren't in extreme distress or haven't died.

Local public health services are now controlling small outbreaks far more cheaply and effectively than T&T. In Darwen in the borough of Blackburn, they created their own system and achieved 90 percent contact tracing in a week – far better than anything T&T has managed. Yet local services have still to see any increase in their funding, whereas £10bn has gone to T&T, with £6.5bn to the private sector and £56m spent on management consultants to make the government's flawed approach smell better.

Strategy, what strategy?

HANCOCK, meanwhile, is building a parallel universe of outsourced mass Covid testing, with pisspoor contact tracing. The NHS and local authorities will then be left to pick up the pieces. Currently, positive tests are up, but hospital admissions and deaths are down. This could be because more people are being tested, more young people are being infected with minimal symptoms or the virus has become less virulent.

Some people who have recovered from Covid and are no longer infectious may also test positive because of tiny fragments of residual RNA amplified in the testing process. You may spot these from the number of test cycles needed to produce a positive test, but private labs don't routinely report this. It requires huge public health expertise to make sense of it all, and to decide if further lockdowns are warranted on the basis of community test results or whether decisions should be made on the basis of hospital admissions and deaths.

Now is probably not the best time to alienate PHE's 5,500 public health experts by announcing in the *Torygraph* that they may lose their jobs. And in choosing Dido Harding (Tory peer and retailer) and Michael Brodie (NHS accountant) as interim chair and CEO of NIHP without a formal selection process, public health expertise looks to be in short supply. The NIHP is already known behind Hancock's back as the National Institute for Self-Protection.

Care home ethics

AS IF care homes haven't suffered enough, many are facing closure as owners see their insurance premiums rise between twofold and eightfold. Insurance is obligatory but, even with the vast hikes, Covid cover is usually not included.

Owners fear they may be sued by relatives for poor infection control if an outbreak occurs, and some homes are keen to market themselves as Covid-free by testing all the residents. However, residents with dementia or learning disability may not have the capacity to consent to the nose and throat swabs the government says they should have every month, and may find the process distressing. It's only legal for a person lacking capacity to have a swab if a doctor deems it to be in his or her best interest (rather than in the interest of the government, care home or community). As one specialist observed: "Many care homes are asking GPs if they can issue a DoLS [deprivation of liberty safeguards] to hold reluctant residents down for a swab. In Croydon, we have decided that no one who objects to swabbing will be swabbed. I'm not sure what others are doing."

Cancer scare

WE HAD a big problem with delayed diagnosis of cancer even before the pandemic, with a 2019 Macmillan Cancer Support assessment putting the UK at the bottom of the table for cancer outcomes in rich nations, and predicting it would miss its 2028 target to catch 75 percent of all cancers in stages one or two. There is a dire shortage of staff to do the screening (eg colonoscopists). Post-pandemic, it's likely that delayed cancer diagnoses, and the avoidable death and disease that results, will overshadow Covid.

A typical district general hospital (DGH) will have a backlog of 10,000 X-ray and scan requests because of Covid, with 1,000 more arriving each week. Staff have to prioritise the most urgent, with one radiologist describing it as "a never-ending treadmill". The only solution the government has to the record waiting times is to transfer another £10bn-worth of treatment from the NHS to the private sector. This won't solve the staffing problem, as many staff flit between sites to serve two masters.

Tweet of the fortnight

THE combined intellects of NHS England and NHS Improvement were keen not to miss an insensitive recruitment opportunity in the A-level results chaos. "If you didn't get the #ALevelResults you were expecting, or perhaps you did but you've changed your mind about the path you'd like to take – it's not too late to apply for a nursing course through #clearing #WeAreTheNHS."

11 & 12 August: Data shows UK employment fell by 730,000 between March and July and UK economy shrank by 20.4 percent between April and June – biggest slump on record. UK death toll falls by more than 5,000 as government changes way deaths are counted. 14 Aug: Fines for not wearing a face mask rise to £3,200. Lockdowns extended in the north-west of England. 17 Aug: England's A-level and GCSE students to be given centre-assessed grades after outcry over results given by algorithm.

MD on The search for safety

Private Eye 1530   Press day: 7 September
2,532 daily cases   **12** daily deaths   **41,554** UK deaths to date

Confidence tricks

"AN ounce of confidence is worth a tonne of taxpayers' money." So proclaimed Boris Johnson in an attempt to justify an end to the furlough scheme, and to bounce Keir Starmer into agreeing it is "safe" for children to return to school and adults to return to work. It all depends how you measure safety...

Based on past performance, it seems reasonable to worry about future safety in a second wave. On 30 August, in the run-up to reopening, even the *Torygraph* gave Johnson a kicking: "Revealed: How, on every measure, Britain's response to the Covid pandemic has been woeful."

In excess deaths per 100,000 people, we are top of Europe, with a double whammy of the highest Covid deaths and highest non-Covid deaths in people too frightened to leave home. The fear of returning to work was hardly helped by Johnson picking up the virus at work (along with numerous colleagues) and needing intensive care. If we couldn't keep our leader safe, what hope is there for a meat factory worker?

Current risk

AT 2,988 confirmed positive tests for Covid in the UK on 6 September, we're still a long way from many public health experts' preferred goal of zero Covid. An ONS sample estimates the "true" number of new infections in England to be up to 4,200 a day. But this is mainly in the under 40s and has not (yet) translated into an increase in hospital admissions and deaths.

Children are as likely to die from a lightning strike as from Covid, and more likely to die in a road traffic accident now schools have reopened. An adult in England currently faces daily risks of a one-in-2,000,000 chance of dying from Covid and a one-in-200,000 chance of surviving with debilitating symptoms of "long Covid". Do you feel lucky? It may well be safer for you to leave home than stay put. Isolation leads to despair. There have been thousands of extra home deaths in the

UK during the pandemic that have yet to be fully explained.

Other risks

INDIVIDUAL Covid risks clearly vary according to age, ethnicity, poverty, working environment, human behaviour and pre-existing medical conditions. And risk is contagious; a US study found that poorer people with Covid were also at double the risk of depression.

In our obsession with Covid, we may still be neglecting other risks that are actually more life threatening. Delays in seeking or getting help for chest pain, stroke or red-flag cancer symptoms (bleeding, lumps, weight loss, night sweats, jaundice, change in bowel habit, pain, etc) markedly worsen the prognosis.

In the week to 14 August, the number of deaths in England and Wales involving Covid-19 decreased for the 17th consecutive week. However, the overall number of deaths registered was 3.4 percent above the five-year average (307 deaths higher). It's likely the hot weather killed far more people than Covid, but there were precious few warnings about how to stay safe in the heat.

Testing times, pt 94

TESTING remains key to picking up future outbreaks, but only if it is followed up by thorough contact tracing and financial support for those forced to isolate for 14 days.

The centralised and outsourced NHS Test and Trace system has not hit its target of 80 percent contact tracing, with local authorities having much more success with less money. They need to be given the

resources to control outbreaks in their communities. This is hampered by a lack of testing capacity in low-prevalence areas (eg London and the South-west), with an algorithm sending people 75 miles as the crow flies for a test, which in reality may be much further. Poorer people are most at risk from Covid and least likely to be able to afford a day trip for a test. As a result, many people with symptoms or those who have been in contact won't be tested. How much simpler if GPs could simply order tests for their patients, particularly those needing the most explanation and support.

Hancock's half-million

MATT HANCOCK's response to test shortcomings is always to announce a huge "high-tech", "world-beating" expansion just around the corner, with 500,000 daily tests now planned by the end of October (more than double the current number; terms and conditions apply). The hope in April was that people could be trusted to test themselves, hence the hundreds of thousands of self-swab kits bought and mailed out at vast expense. Nearly two-thirds of these went undone because samples were either not returned intact or were not returned at all.

The next great hope is that 20-minute-turnaround saliva tests with sufficient specificity and sensitivity are developed – but the focus should still be on testing symptomatic and higher-risk individuals first. Blanket testing of asymptomatic individuals requires consent, and the lower the prevalence of the disease, the more likely false-positive results will cause people – or communities even – to lock down unnecessarily.

"We shouldn't watch the news –
it's just depressing"

It also requires significant resources and personnel that could be used elsewhere (on, say, cancer screening). The bottom line is that it needs to be properly evaluated to ensure it is effective and efficient.

Disunited nations

STRUCTURAL inequalities are at the heart of the world's health problems, but at least the United Nations is trying to do something about them. In 2015 it came up with 17 sustainable development goals (SDGs) to deliver by 2030. As with the 1978 WHO plan of "Health for all by the year 2000", it's proving far easier to persuade member states to sign up for Utopia many years hence than to get them to deliver in the present.

In the first five years, progress was patchy. On the plus side, more children were in school, many infectious diseases were in decline, access to safely managed drinking water had improved, and women's representation in leadership roles was increasing. On the downside, food insecurity was on the rise, the natural environment continued to deteriorate at an alarming rate and high levels of inequality persisted in all regions (including the UK).

The 2030 targets looked doubtful, not least "ending poverty in all its forms everywhere". The current rate of extreme global poverty is 8.2 percent, and even before the pandemic it was felt that only a modest reduction to 6 percent would be possible by 2030. Now it looks set to rise to 8.7 percent. This would mean the first rise in global poverty since 1998, with 71m more people likely to be living in extreme poverty after the pandemic.

Grim reading

THE UN's 2020 SDG update was meant to launch "the decade of action", but it makes pretty grim reading. Seventy countries halted childhood vaccination programmes during the pandemic, and health services for cancer screening, family planning or non-Covid-19 infectious diseases have been interrupted or are being neglected.

Hundreds of thousands of additional deaths under the age of five are now expected in 2020, with a 100 percent increase in malaria deaths in sub-Saharan Africa. Even before the pandemic, less than half the global population was covered by essential health services. In low-income countries, the school completion rate is 34 percent in the poorest 20 percent of households and 79 percent in the richest. As many as 500m students have no access to remote learning. Only 65 percent of primary schools have basic hand-washing facilities. Cases of domestic violence, particularly against women, have increased by 30 percent in some countries during lockdown.

One in five healthcare facilities worldwide has no soap and water or alcohol-based hand rub; 3bn people lack basic hand-washing facilities at home; 789m lack electricity. In some developing countries, one in four healthcare facilities does not have electricity.

On a brighter note, Covid may result in a 6 percent fall in greenhouse gas emissions for 2020 – but this is still short of the 7.6 percent annual reduction needed to limit global warming to 1.5°C.

---

27 August: WHO says an expert team will visit Wuhan to study origins of Covid-19. **28 Aug**: Government announces another drive to encourage people to return to their workplaces. **30 Aug**: Global cases pass 25m. India sets unwanted world record of 78,761 confirmed cases in 24 hours. In the UK, the University and College Union warns against university campuses reopening in September. **31 Aug**: Eat Out to Help Out ends, having subsidised more than 100m meals at a cost of £522m. **1 September**: Most schools in England, Wales and Northern Ireland reopen. **4 Sept**: WHO says widespread vaccination will not be possible until mid-2021.

GOVERNMENT GUIDANCE

GOVERNMENT POLICY

MD on Covid's second wave

Private Eye 1531   Press day: 21 September

4,964 daily cases   **28** daily deaths   **41,788** UK deaths to date

Living with Covid

THE combination of increased social interaction and test and trace failure has accelerated the second wave of Covid, and the dilemma facing the government. Should we try another lockdown, at huge personal cost, or learn to live with Covid, as we do with other viruses? In an ideal world, the focus should be on protecting those at higher risk, while allowing those at lower risk to sensibly work, study and play. For any strategy to work, we need a functional test and trace system, clear messaging and widespread public compliance. We currently lack all three.

Clueless

PUTTING a rookie health secretary and a mobile phone retailer in charge of a public health emergency was always a high-risk strategy, but for NHS Test and Trace boss Dido Harding to claim that "nobody was expecting the really sizeable increase in demand for tests" in September is beyond clueless. Harding even had the gall to blame SAGE, the scientific advisory group for emergencies, for not warning her.

Matt Hancock's excuse for the shortages and delayed reporting is that people are demanding tests "inappropriately" because they are free (as if anyone enjoys driving hundreds of miles with a car-sick child to gag on a long swab). In fact, the large surge in demand was both predicted and predictable. Here are some of the clues...

1) The fact that people would be returning to work, school and university all at the same time was highly suggestive of an increase in viral spread and test demands in September.

2) All sorts of other microbes are spread between pupils, students and workers at this time of year, many causing similar symptoms to Covid and further increasing demand for tests.

3) On 31 July, chief medical officer Professor Chris Whitty warned that the country had already "reached the limit" for opening up society.

We were nowhere near zero Covid and an autumn uprising was on the cards. "If people continue to increase their number of social interactions, the virus rates will go up absolutely inevitably. We've got to stop now – we may have to pull back a bit, in fact, to keep this under control."

4) When asked on the *Today* programme on 1 August whether pubs could have to shut for schools to reopen, Prof Graham Medley, chair of the SAGE sub-group on pandemic modelling, said: "I think that's quite possible… Closing other networks may well be required to enable us to open schools. It might come down to a trade-off… Do we think pubs are more important than schools?"

5) We ploughed ahead opening up everything, and turbocharged it with the hugely popular "Eat Out to Help Out" scheme, cramming people into pubs and restaurants to pick up the virus just before returning to school, work and university.

6) Those returning from countries experiencing surges of infection understandably want to know if they've brought the virus back with them. Hence more demand for tests.

7) In August, SAGE advised the government that only "around 20 percent of those reporting symptoms of Covid-19 in England report fully self-isolating by staying at home". Many airport arrivals have not properly quarantined. People have celebrated summer and the end of lockdown by shunning social distancing and masks, getting pissed and partying. On "non-compliance" grounds alone, a September surge was highly likely.

8) Hancock and PM Boris Johnson have continually boasted about their "world-class" test and trace system, and their Moonshot plan for "on the spot" testing to be made available for anyone who wants it. This may have led people to believe that anyone who wants a test can get it.

9) In July, Test and Trace supremo Harding advised anyone who "just wasn't feeling right" to get a test.

10) Up to 10 percent of those infected experience long Covid symptoms that may be indistinguishable from the initial infection. They are likely to seek another test to see if they have been re-infected.

11) Anxiety levels are very high, particularly about the return to school and work, and anxiety alone can mimic and accentuate all manner of symptoms, driving demands for tests. If you can't get a test, the anxiety and the symptoms get worse.

We have a problem...

PANDEMICS spread like bushfires. Outbreaks start as multiple small fires, which join together if you don't extinguish them. Once again, we haven't managed to extinguish them.

The government took the view that people needed to enjoy the freedom of Sweden over the summer to offset the side effects of prolonged lockdown (depression, anxiety, poverty, domestic abuse, vitamin D deficiency, etc.) However, we lack the space and social responsibility of Sweden, so instead of getting close to zero Covid over summer, as the Swedes have managed, we were always destined to take a high loading dose into September. There is no excuse for not planning ahead.

Staff in care homes and hospitals are already reporting test shortages, and some care homes have been asked to accept infected residents back from hospital. Hospital and ITU admissions with Covid are up. We know where this is heading. At least 620 UK health and care workers died in wave one, and anxiety and burnout levels are high. Let's hope PPE stocks are also high.

On a brighter note...

WE have become much better at treating serious Covid, with drugs and ITU techniques that have reduced mortality substantially. We lack testing capacity but have far more than in March. We must now target the available testing where it's most needed. Luckily, this virus is relatively harmless to the vast majority of people. If you're fit and under 65, you're as likely to be killed by your morning commute by car as by the virus, although if you do get it, there's a 10 percent chance you'll experience unpleasant symptoms for at least three weeks. If you get new symptoms, it's much easier to do the right thing to control the virus if you have easy access to tests and quick results. In the absence of this, can you tell if your symptoms are Covid-related or not?

Ask an app?

THE Covid-19 Symptom Study App has data from 4,223,009 citizens in the UK (including MD), and has been given a £2m government grant. Its data shows infection can be hard to spot. On 2 August, it declared that around a fifth of adults who had been infected had no symptoms.

Adults have a much greater range of Covid symptoms (20) than the three the government has highlighted (high temperature, persistent cough and loss of smell or taste). Indeed, 27 percent of those found to have Covid didn't have any of the government's three "core" symptoms. These were often elderly patients, most at risk, who often just "felt awful". They also tend to "feel awful" when they have a heart attack, cancer or a bowel obstruction, which may explain why so many died at home of potentially treatable non-Covid conditions.

According to the app, the top Covid symptoms for adults are fatigue (87 percent), headache (72 percent), loss of smell (60 percent), persistent cough (54 percent) and sore throat (49 percent). The advice from researchers at King's College London in August was the same as Harding's: "If you have any symptoms you can't explain, get a test."

Children are different

CHILDREN are far more likely to be harmed by missing school than contracting Covid, and their symptoms are also differ from those of adults.

Fifty-two percent of school-aged children who tested positive for Covid didn't experience cough, fever or loss of smell in the weeks before and after the test, and a third who tested positive didn't log any symptoms at all. The top five symptoms for Covid-positive children were fatigue (55 percent) headache (53 percent), fever (49 percent), sore throat (38 percent) and loss of appetite (35 percent). One in six (15 percent) had an unusual skin rash. Other presentations include diarrhoea, vomiting and abdominal pain. Given the wide range of possible symptoms, it's very hard to know if your child has Covid or appendicitis without taking a test.

Covid roulette

NOW that testing has gone tits-up just when we need it, we are left with Covid roulette. So what are the possible outcomes if we continue to mingle?

Option 1: Take all precautions, don't get the virus. A good result. That's what I'm aiming for.

Option 2: Get the virus, fully recover, don't pass it on. Also a good result. You add to herd immunity, at least for a while.

Option 3: Get the virus, pass it on to others at low risk who all recover fully without killing anyone. Again, a good option that boosts herd immunity and so protects the vulnerable, but very hard to pull off.

Option 4: Get the virus, kill Granny. Probably a bad outcome, depending on your relationship with your grandmother and whether she wants to die.

Option 5: Get the virus, get long Covid. Bad luck.

Option 6: Death. Very bad luck in the under-65s but a merciful release in the over-95s.

Option 7: Fall down the stairs while vision obscured by face mask. Not unknown.

Option 8: Operation Moonshot. Test 10m random people a day from January. This could lead to 230,000 citizens with false-positive results wrongly self-isolating every day, and cost the taxpayer £100bn. As with all of medicine, more is not always better.

Option 9: Hand back Serco and Sitel Test and Trace to the NHS. This hugely expensive outsourcing didn't predict the second wave and isn't delivering. Time to put local public health experts in charge of local outbreaks.

---

9 September: Gatherings of more than six to be banned from 14 Sept, amid fears of second wave. Government hopes "Operation Moonshot" mass testing programme will help avoid a second lockdown. **11 Sept:** R number estimated at 1.0–1.2 for first time since March. **14 Sept:** Chief scientific adviser Sir Patrick Vallance says he was rebuked by officials for favouring lockdown early in the pandemic. WHO predicts Europe will see rise in cases in October and November. **17 Sept:** France records new high of more than 10,000 daily cases, as WHO warns of "alarming rates of transmission" in Europe. **19 Sept:** BMA calls for tighter restrictions in England. **21 Sept:** UK coronavirus alert upgraded to level 4, meaning transmission is "high or rising exponentially".

HOKUSAI'S SECOND WAVE

MD on The bigger picture

Private Eye 1532   Press day: 5 October

14,520 daily cases   **56** daily deaths   **42,369** UK deaths to date

How others do it

WILD spread of Covid-19 is slowed by doing the basics: hands, face, space and indoor ventilation. Because so much spread is asymptomatic, it is vital to stamp on symptomatic infections as soon as they occur. The UK's test and trace system can't cope. It has rationed tests so thousands can't get them and delayed contact tracing of more than 15,000 positive tests by up to 10 days because of a "computer glitch". So up soars the wild spread.

Most countries with a grip on the virus without lockdowns have ruthless test and trace systems. Testing, reporting, tracing and quarantining are all done at high speed, with high efficiency. The poor are supported to isolate. There is a focus on breaking chains of transmission. Each new case is treated as if it were the first. Levels of public trust and compliance are high because public services are efficient. You get your Covid test result back so quickly, you know you're positive before you travel from Scotland to Westminster to spray saliva at colleagues and the common people.

Dear Mr Hancock...

MANY GPs are witnessing the wider harm to their patients of lockdown. London GP and *Eye* reader Dr Ellie Cannon has written to Matt Hancock asking him to take a more holistic and nuanced approach to pandemic management. More than 60 GPs (and MD) have countersigned.

"From the outset, the chief medical officer has spoken of four different categories of harm from the pandemic, correctly warning of non-Covid or 'indirect' deaths due to pandemic measures and downscaling of healthcare. Speaking to the House of Commons science and technology committee on 24 April 2020 Prof Whitty also highlighted that 'if as a result of economic downturn for prolonged periods deprivation increases, that will have a health effect'.

"As a group of expert medical generalists, we urgently wish you to consider non-Covid harms and deaths with equal standing as the reported deaths from Covid," the letter states. "We fully supported the first lockdown when little was known about the virus. The position now is transformationally different: after the short, initial lockdown phase, the harms to long-term health and wellbeing begin to outweigh the benefits...

"The one-track response threatens more lives and livelihoods than Covid-lives saved. A total of 30,260 excess deaths have occurred in private homes since March, but less than 1 in 10 are due to Covid-19.

"The pandemic has resulted in an inflation of acute cardiovascular deaths, most of which did not relate to Covid-19. There is a concerning signal that child suicide death rates in the UK increased during lockdown; and amongst those reported after lockdown, restriction to education and other activities, disruption to care and support services, tensions at home and isolation appeared to be contributing factors.

"The older shielding population with multiple long-term health conditions (the very group whom restrictions were aimed at protecting) experienced higher levels of depression, anxiety and loneliness compared with those who were not shielding and were more likely to be less physically active than usual. Covid deaths alone can no longer be used as the unilateral measure of harm [...] We do not wish to undermine the seriousness of pandemic management but the wider harm to babies, children, young people and adults of all ages can no longer be ignored."

Do the least harm

IT's impossible to "do no harm" in a pandemic, but we could at least try to do the least harm. But first, we have to measure it.

We can measure unemployment, suicide, welfare benefits and waiting times for cancer and heart disease treatment. We can do regular surveys of mental health, check literacy and numeracy, log concerns from social workers, health and care staff and teachers, and calls to domestic abuse helplines and Childline. We can measure muscle mass, malnutrition, falls, fractures and fitness levels in the elderly locked indoors. We can see how few job vacancies there are and how applicants per post have risen sharply.

We know our response to Covid has cost around £370bn, and that public sector debt has exceeded GDP for the first time since the early 1960s. We can measure GDP (11.7 percent smaller than it was pre-lockdown), we know a third of jobs were furloughed at some point, with the young most affected, and we can count how many turn out to be "non-viable". And we can count deaths.

Dying at home

OF THE 30,260 "excess" deaths – that is, above the five-year average expectation – in private homes since March, less than 1 in 10 is attributed to Covid-19. We don't know why.

It might be because patients weren't seen or tested. Many can't drive to a not-so-near test centre and others are declined a test as "ineligible". Frail older people are most at risk of death from any cause, including Covid. They often don't have classic symptoms of any disease and just feel dreadful. The excellent Covid Symptom Tracker App (Zoe) found that the key Covid symptom in the elderly is delirium – a new, confused mental state – which won't qualify them for a test. So those most at risk from Covid are least likely to get diagnosis and treatment.

Each week 12,000 people die in the UK, many from conditions more treatable or preventable than Covid. It could be that thousands have died from cardiac conditions at home who might have been saved in hospital. We do few post-mortems, especially at the moment, so will never know for sure (a lucky escape for the government). But many consultants are anxious about reductions in cancer and cardiac events reaching hospital. Hence the hard sell that "the NHS is open for all business".

Student health

HALLS of residence are high risk for Covid. Countless public health experts warned that student migration would lead to outbreaks. We also know that the risk of death from Covid if you're under 24 is less than the risk from falling down the stairs.

The virus is still best avoided because of post-viral syndromes, but students – especially freshers – are at greater risk of anxiety, depression and self-harm, and locking them down may have increased those risks further while exposing them to their flatmate's virus. Was this wise?

Teachers' health

SCHOOL staff may be at higher risk of exposure now, but there is wide variability in how "Covid-safe" schools (and workplaces) are. In some schools, the windows don't open. In others, you're not allowed to open the windows. In some, the windows are always open but you're not allowed to wear a coat if you're freezing. The statistics suggest school spread is currently low. However, some staff will be harmed by occupational exposure. And pupils are harmed when schools are closed. Where do we strike the balance?

App-etizer

MD downloaded the belated NHS Covid App immediately and has been wandering around Somerset with it on. If I get pinged, I will do as instructed. I don't want to get Covid and I don't want to pass it on. However, with modest restrictions, it is still possible to enjoy life and have five portions of fun a day. The app would be even more useful if it told you the local restrictions in different regions and if someone in your pub should be isolating. It doesn't have to identify him. But it probably is a him.

The Covid cube

THE Covid cube is a fiendishly hard puzzle to solve. We've got a virus that 90 percent of people haven't yet had. Of the 10 percent who have, many don't realise it. Just 20 percent of people may account for 80 percent of the spread. The vast majority aren't harmed but the unlucky few suffer lung and heart damage, clots and strokes, extreme fatigue and death.

We need a ruthlessly efficient test and trace system that tests frontline health and care staff every week. At present we have the highest Covid death toll, the highest non-Covid death toll and the biggest educational and economic hit in Europe. So who to blame?

Freedom-loving Brits?

PEER-reviewed research published in *Public Health* has found that in early May, at the height of pandemic deaths, only 18 percent of people self-isolated properly after developing symptoms. Only 11 percent quarantined properly after being in contact with a confirmed case.

Non-compliance was high in all social groups. Men and people who didn't think they were much at risk were least likely to do the right thing, but also "non-adherence was associated with having a dependent child in the household, lower socio-economic grade, greater hardship during the pandemic, and working in a key sector".

Blaming citizens for outbreaks is a risky political strategy when you've enthusiastically endorsed Eat Out to Help Out, before encouraging the country to go back to school, university and work all at the same time. The public appear to support stricter measures, probably because they know how many people are not doing what they claim to be supporting. Alas, both the pandemic and the blunter measures used to control it selectively harm the most deprived. All the lockdowns and 83 percent of Covid hospital deaths are currently in the North and Midlands. We may be in the same storm but we are on very different boats.

---

22 September: UK records highest daily tally of cases since May. **25 Sept**: The R number rises from 1.1–1.4 to 1.2–1.5. Official figures show the UK borrowed £35.9bn in August to tackle economic fallout of Covid. **26 Sept**: PM pledges £500m to the Covax global vaccine sharing scheme. **27 Sept**: Wales announces local lockdowns. **28 Sept**: Lockdown is tightened in north-east England. **2 October**: President Donald Trump admitted to hospital less than 24 hours after testing positive. **4 Oct**: Global cases pass 35m. **5 Oct**: Donald Trump leaves hospital. In the UK, an error means 50,000 contacts may not have been traced.

"That's a concerning growth"

MD on Failing better

Private Eye 1533   Press day: 19 October

19,553 daily cases   **151** daily deaths   **43,726** UK deaths to date

We are not alone...

LIKE the UK, many countries are experiencing a second wave of SARS-CoV-2 infection, even Germany. It's hardly surprising as the virus spreads invisibly in the air and on fingers, often asymptomatically. It will wax and wane for some while yet, particularly indoors and in poor ventilation.

In the first wave, the UK came near the bottom of the Euro league for preventing both Covid deaths and harms *and* non-Covid deaths and harms. There have been almost 800 excess deaths from heart and circulatory diseases in people aged under 65 since the pandemic began, perhaps because they were unable or unwilling to seek treatment.

The latest analysis of 21 industrialised countries published in *Nature Medicine* put England and Wales second (behind Spain) in per capita excess deaths between mid-February and May, with a 37 percent increase from the five-year average. Scotland was fourth. As the senior author, Professor Majid Ezzati, put it: "We cannot dismantle the health system through austerity and then expect it to serve people when the need is at its highest, especially in poor and marginalised communities."

The chance of the UK now topping any table for good performance in the second wave would be extremely unlikely. The best we can hope for is to fail better.

An unbeatable virus?

IN JANUARY, MD thought a pandemic could be prevented because the SARS virus would behave like the 2003 version. I couldn't have been more wrong. SARS-CoV-1 was actually more virulent than its successor. But it was less infectious, and infections were easier to spot and contain because they usually involved obvious symptoms, and that is when most spreading occurred.

This year's SARS is a bugger to control because some spread occurs pre-symptomatically and most of those infected have no or minimal symptoms and come to no or minimal harm. This makes it doubly difficult to identify spreaders and persuade them to make big sacrifices for others that may involve considerable health and economic self-harm, and possibly job loss.

Catch-a-virus 22

IF a harmful, contagious virus gets out of control (again), you have to act. But your actions may not work or may do more harm than good. More people may die or be harmed from non-Covid causes than Covid, and lockdowns may worsen public health and immunity so people come to more harm if they do catch the virus.

Worse, we don't have much solid evidence to support any course of action in the long term, or reliably predict the benefits, risks and alternatives. It's a huge gamble with no obvious winner. No matter what your favourite expert says (there are no true experts in pandemics; just expertise in myriad disciplines), decisions are riddled with uncertainty. The known unknowns are overwhelming, never mind the unknown unknowns. It's the mother-of-all Catch 22s.

Learning from the best

TO CONTROL a pandemic, you need a world class test and trace system and world class public compliance. We have neither. As a safety net, you need world class levels of public fitness, so more people make full recoveries from infection, and world class health services that can cope with a surge of infection without closing down the non-infection work. And you need a world class welfare state to help the long-term sick and unemployed. As Boris Johnson has discovered, merely calling something "world class" doesn't make it so.

The British position

THERE are some things we should have fixed in the first lockdown (like emerging with a fully functional, joined-up test, trace, isolate and support system) and some things we couldn't fix that quickly.

Waiting times and health and social care staff shortages were at an all-time high before the pandemic and have grown worse. We built all these amazing Nightingale hospitals that could have been used as "fever hospitals" to allow the rest of the NHS to focus on non-Covid work, but we couldn't staff them. So they were barely used.

The health of the nation is also poor. The virus is more likely to harm those with chronic disease and frailty, and there are 15 million such people in the UK. It is impossible to shield so many and, even if we could, many would refuse to be shielded. We are not China, but we do do lockdowns.

The lockdown paradox

LOCKDOWN is seen as a last resort that proves you have failed in the basics of public health. If you can't put out the fires of infection before they spread out of control, you flood an entire community, drowning those who can't swim. And the later you leave lockdown, the longer it takes to work. Non-Covid harms rise dramatically and people are so stir crazy by the time they get out, they ignore all the rules in favour of human company.

We know this from lockdown number one. It did rapidly cut transmission for a short while, but now we're back where we started. Do we twist or stick, go regional or national?

Regional or national?

LABOUR's Keir Starmer is siding with SAGE and a two- to three-week national circuit-breaker lockdown for the whole of England, similar to the Welsh "fire-break" that adds the cherry of denying English entry from high risk areas. Boris Johnson favours a regional approach that is proportionate to the current levels of prevalence. Neither will work if they are introduced too late (SAGE advised a break on 20 September; Starmer's suggestion of overlapping with half-term is too late). More pertinently, if testing, tracing and public compliance don't improve dramatically, we'll be back where we started within a month of stopping.

Meanwhile, Chris Whitty, England's chief medical officer, believes the regional tier system won't be enough, but has assured us "we will be better at dealing with the virus next winter".

Herd immunity mirage

HERD immunity means getting the R number below 1 permanently, without the need for control measures. Generally, it requires a vaccine and even then you get outbreaks if vaccine levels drop, the virus mutates or immunity is only transient.

The mirage of herd immunity often happens temporarily. Things seemed to go swimmingly in the summer when the R number was below 1; but our over-confidence turbo-charged the second wave. Holidays abroad, Eat Out to Help Out, sending schools, universities and workers back all at the same time – the mirage soon vanished.

Get fit for life

NOBODY knows how this virus will behave in future, but we do know our chances of being harmed by it are higher if we have one or more chronic diseases and obesity.

On 20 September, SAGE published a lengthy analysis of "non-pharmacological interventions", including the "circuit break". However, it completely omitted lifestyle modifications that would not only improve Covid recovery but also reduce the risk of the far more common non-Covid harms, from cancer and diabetes to heart disease, stroke and mental illness. There is very strong evidence of health improvements from stopping smoking, cutting alcohol, better sleep, better diet, regular relaxation and exercise. No drug comes near to matching these benefits. For a fraction of the cost of containing Covid, we could have improved the health of the poorest: big increases in years of healthy living; fewer premature deaths from just about all causes.

Risk communication

RISK communication has been poor in this pandemic. Relentlessly focusing on a single cause of death leads to woeful risk management. Daily Covid deaths not only need to be presented in the context of deaths from other causes, but we also need to know the "years of life lost".

Many of the excess cardiac deaths have been in the under 65s, but the average age of a Covid death is 82.4 years, above the average life expectancy. It may well be that Covid deaths have zero effect on average life expectancy, whereas the preventable non-Covid deaths from cancer, heart disease and miscarriage do.

Isolation help

FEWER than 20 percent of people are isolating properly, and all other measures will fail unless we fix this. Individuals and regions simply will not comply if they struggle to put food on the table or fear losing work.

Going door to door and supporting people to do the right thing is tough, demanding frontline work. Local authorities that have cracked it are using local people with contact tracing expertise and local knowledge. The exclusion of GPs from testing and tracing has been a huge error. The £12bn outsourcing bill invested locally could have delivered better results and left permanent structural improvements in public services. But this government prefers to fund the private sector and management consultants.

Kindness and self-care

THE government clearly isn't capable of protecting your health, but you are. If you can, try to get outside, stay active, socialise safely, eat food that's delicious and nutritious, take vitamin D, have five portions of fun a day, relax and sleep well. If you live in a lower risk area, you might frequent local cafés, pubs and restaurants, but follow the rules. Well ventilated venues are safest. If you're shitting blood or have a new lump, ring your doctor.

If you don't have long to live, make up your own rules. Twenty-eight thousand more deaths have happened at home this year, partly because people don't want to be separated at the end of life. Who can blame them?

At 58, MD is the average age of a Covid ITU admission, and I'm taking all sensible measures to avoid infection. However, my personal risk of heart disease, stroke, cancer and mental illness is far higher. Life is about balancing all sorts of personal risks and then helping those who are less fortunate. For every decision, think: "Is it intelligent? Is it kind?"

---

7 October: Scotland bans indoor drinking in licensed premises for 16 days.
11 Oct: UK records 224,000 new coronavirus cases in a week. Deputy chief medical officer Jonathan Van Tam says UK is at the "tipping point" of the crisis.
12 Oct: New three-tier system of restrictios announced for England, with many northern regions immediately entering higher tiers. **13 Oct**: Labour leader Keir Starmer calls for "circuit-breaker" lockdown. **17 Oct**: World sees a record 400,000 cases in one day. Wales to enter a two-week circuit-breaker lockdown from 23 Oct. London, Essex and York enter Tier 2. **19 Oct**: Chief scientific adviser says UK won't get a Covid-19 vaccine until spring.

MD on How to defeat Covid

Private Eye **1534**   **Press day: 2 November**

22,551 daily cases   **309** daily deaths   **46,853** UK deaths to date

The nuclear option

IS a month of another lockdown long enough to get the virus under control in the UK? And how will we keep it there? Boris Johnson made no mention of fixing test and trace at his press conference, preferring to fantasise about imminent vaccines, better drugs and the army delivering 15-minute self-test kits to "whole cities" "within days". But is there an existing route map out of the pandemic that avoids lockdowns, excess deaths and economic carnage? Step forward Taiwan…

The Taiwan way

THE SARS-CoV-2 virus may be rising again across Europe and America, but Taiwan hasn't had a locally transmitted infection for more than 200 days. This is all the more surprising given that it's a crowded democratic island of 23m people off the coast of China, with direct flights to Wuhan and many densely populated cities. Many residents live close together in apartments. In SARS 2003, it was the third worst affected country. Yet in 2020 it has had only 555 confirmed cases and seven deaths, with no lockdowns and no second wave.

Equally impressive, GDP is predicted to grow by 1.56 percent in 2020 and life is near to normal. On 8 August, Taiwanese singer-songwriter Eric Chou held a concert at Taipei Arena for more than 10,000 people, indoors and with no social distancing enforced. No outbreak followed. Sports, music, shopping, dining, drinking and dancing venues are at full capacity. How?

The scars of SARS

TAIWAN began building an emergency-response network for containing infectious diseases after SARS in 2003, which also originated in China and was more lethal than the current version but less infectious. As a result, countries closest to China bore the brunt, with Taiwan having hundreds of cases and 73 deaths. Hospitals had to be barricaded off. It became clear that unconstitutional emergency measures might be needed at the first signs of a pandemic and the habits of handwashing and mask-wearing became widely accepted, further reinforced by bird and swine flu outbreaks.

Sunflower Movement

IN Taiwan, people are used to living under high alert. Beijing has more than 1,600 ballistic missiles pointed at their island. In spring 2014, student protesters took to the streets in Taipei after outrage at the incumbent KMT Nationalist Party's attempt to fast-track a trade deal with China. This "Sunflower Movement" continued into the 2016 election and helped the Democratic Progressive Party (DPP) win power, with academic Tsai Ing-wen becoming Taiwan's first female president. Public trust in her leadership has been crucial to Taiwan's pandemic success.

Crack hacker

EQUALLY crucial to the country's success is digital minister Audrey Tang. Tang, a civic hacker, was working in Silicon Valley when the Sunflower protests started but returned home to set up broadband connections and a digital strategy that helped the protesters win the political argument. On gaining power, the DPP appointed Tang as digital minister and used her expertise to crowd-source and share opinions to inform government policy. This civic digital democracy has been central to getting public support for pandemic measures and in supporting people to follow the rules.

Listen to whistleblowers

WHEN Chinese physician Dr Li Wenliang blew the whistle on the outbreak of a new SARS-like virus in Wuhan at the end of December 2019, his warning was reposted by a citizen on a Taiwanese civic network and taken seriously. In January, Taiwan set up a Central Epidemic Command Center (CECC) even before Wuhan went into lockdown. It introduced travel restrictions and set up quarantine protocols for high-risk travellers. Flights from Wuhan were suspended.

Border control

AS an island nation, Taiwan realised immediate and lasting border control was the best chance of keeping the virus out. It was right. Today, and for the foreseeable future, it has a 14-day quarantine from all destinations for all arrivals, whether Taiwanese or foreign. There is "symptom-based surveillance" before travellers board flights. Arrivals can choose to go to a hotel for 14 days of physical quarantine or stay in their own homes if they have their own bathroom and put their phones into the "digital quarantine", which tracks movements. They get US$33 per day as a stipend, but if they break the quarantine they are fined a thousand times that. Compliance is very high, as much from public support as fear of a fine. And Taiwan provides meal and grocery deliveries for those quarantining and friendly contact via Line Bot, a robot that texts and chats.

Track & trace, Taiwan-style

TAIWAN was ahead of the game going into the pandemic. In 2017, in response to the Ebola outbreak in West Africa, its centre for disease control developed a comprehensive, digital national contact tracing platform (TRACE). This was adapted for Covid in mid-January, and by the time the first infected person was discovered on 21 January, it was possible to track the travel and contact history of every single patient.

This kept the outbreak manageable, allowing nearly all contacts to be traced, which in turn kept the numbers low – a virtuous circle, only possible thanks to immediate action before infections got out of control and widespread public support. The more successful track and trace is, the more public support it gets. People allow their phones to be tracked because it gets results.

For each confirmed case, 20-30 contacts have been reached; 340,000 people have been under home quarantine, with fewer than 1,000 fined for breaking it – an impressive 99.7 percent compliance. As health minister Chen Shih-chung says: "We sacrificed 14 days of 340,000 people in exchange for normal lives for 23m people."

Trust the people

THEY have also been clever in Taiwan in places where people are warier of tracing, such as nightclubs and bars. Based on work with HIV-positive communities, they trusted venues to come up with their own contact tracing systems using codenames, single-use email or prepaid mobile phone numbers. This avoided data being sent to central government.

Public trust is also high because digital networks are used to ensure transparency and information flows from the top down and the bottom up. Tang and fellow hacktivists have set up vTaiwan, an online democracy and brainstorming site, to involve citizens rather than just dictating rules to them. Public involvement has improved the pandemic response and nurtured civic pride.

Humour, not rumour

TAIWAN has three pillars to its pandemic response: fair, fast and (surprisingly) fun. Rather than scaring the shit out of citizens with relentless killer virus death statistics, it uses humour: a cute dog called Zongchai, a shiba inu, which translates key messages into easily understandable pictures. For physical distancing, the caption says: "If you're outdoors, please keep two shiba inus away... If you're indoors, keep three shiba inus away from each other." Maybe you have to be there, but it seems to work.

Humour is also used to stamp out fake news and conspiracy theories. One rumour, started by a toilet roll manufacturer, was that shops would run out because the same paper was being used to make face masks. In response, Tang's team released a meme featuring Taiwan's premier Su Tseng-chang with the caption "we only have one pair of buttocks". It stated that the pulp in toilet paper was from South America and mask materials were all locally sourced. The meme spread much faster than the conspiracy, and ridiculous over-buying of bog roll stopped.

National health system

TAIWAN has a well-funded and efficient single-payer health system covering the entire population. Unlike in the UK, citizens do not live in fear of accessing medical care in case they pick up Covid. In Taiwan there have been no waves of non-Covid deaths either. People with cancer and heart disease feel safe to seek help, and the health system is not overloaded. Taiwan has much to teach the world, and the World Health Organization, but is currently excluded from the WHO (and the UN) because China, the WHO's second biggest funder, claims to "speak for Taiwan". Any WHO sanctioned inquiry into the pandemic must include evidence and lessons from Taiwan, separate from any Chinese testimony. [*Note: Despite doing brilliantly throughout 2020, even Taiwan relaxed too soon, and by spring 2021 it too had taken a hit.*]

Suppress or simmer?

TAIWAN has a third the population of the UK so copying its suppression strategies would be more complex and may not succeed. Great Britain and Ireland are islands, and so could enforce Taiwan-style border quarantines but have chosen not to. New Zealand and Australia have much stricter border controls which allow citizens far more freedom within them. Local outbreaks still happen, but Victoria managed to suppress 700 new cases a day to less than a case a day. As they go into summer, the virus should be easier to control.

We let the virus simmer over summer, rather than suppress it, with patchy testing and poor public compliance. So the second wave is much bigger than it needed to be.

Can T&T be fixed?

SUPPRESSING a highly infectious virus that spreads without symptoms in sudden waves is extremely hard, and probably not possible without border quarantines to keep new outbreaks at a traceable level. Across Europe, T&T systems have failed to suppress a second wave. In the UK, £12bn has been spent on a largely outsourced system, but the message that local tracing gets better results is filtering through. More than 100 local councils in England now have "tracing partnerships" with Public Health England. They should provide financial and social support, and access to food or medicines. Local authorities know where their pockets of hunger and poverty are and urgently need resources to tackle them.

Local tracing is funded from a share of £300m government funding plus £8 per head for enhanced tracing and enforcement in areas under higher-tier restrictions – a fraction of what the private sector has been given. Local authorities must be fully funded to trace and support, with the help of local NHS and GPs, so when the numbers come down to a manageable level again, we can keep them there.

Next time we have to suppress, not simmer.

Waiting for utopia

GLOBAL herd immunity is the utopia of public health. It means enough people on the planet are immune to a disease, either via vaccine or exposure, to allow those who are still susceptible to travel freely without getting infected. Herd immunity could theoretically happen with SARS-CoV-2. And if we find a vaccine that works, we wouldn't have to vaccinate the entire population, just enough to keep the R number below 1. However, even when epidemics appear to have ended, they can fire up again quickly, seemingly at random. No one is out of the woods yet.

---

20 October: Government forces tighter restrictions on Greater Manchester after failing to reach agreement with local politicians. **28 Oct**: France and Germany impose month-long lockdowns. **29 Oct**: Imperial College London estimates there are 100,000 new cases in England each day, with the number doubling every nine days. **31 Oct**: PM announces four-week national lockdown in England, to start on 5 November, to prevent a "medical and moral disaster" for NHS. Schools, universities and courts to remain open. Furlough scheme extended until December. Total confirmed UK cases passes 1m; US total passes 9m.

"This is the living room, and the
playroom, and the classroom, and the
gym, and the office, and the…"

MD on Why the UK is banking on a vaccine

Private Eye 1535   Press day: 16 November

23,294 daily cases   **407** daily deaths   **52,147** UK deaths to date

Turkish delight

DOMINIC CUMMINGS' Brexit "success" was partially built on the, er, lie that millions of Turkish immigrants were heading for the UK. In other news, the children of Turkish immigrants to Germany have developed a vaccine that could control the pandemic.

BioNTech was founded by husband and wife team Prof Ugur Sahin and Dr Özlem Türeci, who put their livelihoods on the line to develop mRNA vaccine technology and even spent their wedding day in the lab. When they started to be successful, US drug giant Pfizer stepped in to help with development, marketing, profiteering and distribution. The UK has bought 40 million doses, to be made in Germany and Belgium. It has to be stored at -70°C and delivery is time and temperature critical. Let's hope nothing in January 2021 impedes the free and fast movement of EU goods across our border…

Vaccine to the rescue?

THE world would be less populated and less travelled without the vaccines that prevent cholera, diphtheria, hepatitis, Japanese encephalitis, measles, meningitis, mumps, pertussis, pneumonia, polio, rabies, rotavirus, rubella, tetanus, tuberculosis, typhoid, varicella, yellow fever, ano-genital and cervical cancer and warts. The fact that only one infectious disease has been eliminated (smallpox) shows how hard it is to defeat microbes, but vaccines have enhanced and prolonged the lives of hundreds of millions. As UK Covid deaths exceed 50,000, the news that safe and effective vaccines for SARS-CoV-2 may soon be with us is cause for cautious celebration. It might even save prime minister Boris Johnson's career.

Mandatory v. voluntary

IN SOME countries vaccination may be mandatory, and it may be compulsory for those wishing to travel to them. In the UK, vaccination should remain voluntary. Forcing any treatment on a competent adult against their will would set a dangerous precedent.

Informed consent is key. Individuals who opt in may have individual protection for as long as the vaccine lasts, but more lasting population protection will require a majority of citizens to consent to it. However, 36 percent of people in the UK and 51 percent in the US report being either uncertain or unlikely to agree to be vaccinated against the coronavirus, according to a report by the British Academy and the Royal Society. Given such widespread vaccine hesitancy, accuracy of information and trust in those giving it will be crucial.

Statistical approval

THE UK government burned its trust boats over Brexit, when bias, lies and bluster triumphed over balanced argument. Its handling of Covid has been dangerously incompetent. Recently it was criticised by the UK Statistics Authority for making overblown claims about testing capacity, not being transparent in its data and getting slides wrong. As the government lurches from fear to hope, it needs to get a grip on its information giving. Statistics and slides should be independently pre-approved by the Office for National Statistics. Drug companies, too, must be exemplary in the way they release data on vaccines.

Great expectations... and profits

THE headline of "90 percent effective" for the Pfizer BioNTech vaccine (BNT162b2) is good news, but this should have waited until all the data had been independently verified in a peer review journal. Instead, we got a press release with scant data.

It was "a great day for science and humanity", said Albert Bourla, Pfizer's chairman and chief executive. It was certainly a great day for Bourla, who had scheduled the sale of 130,000 of his Pfizer shares that day and made £5.6m as the price rocketed. Chief corporate affairs officer Sally Susman also cashed in shares. All legal, but appearance is everything and this was more grist to the anti-vaxxers' mill.

If a company produces a vaccine that gets the pandemic under control, it deserves its profits. But for the boss to cash in before it has been tried in the real world suggests it might not stand up to the competition.

Russia then trumped America by announcing its Sputnik-V vaccine has a "92 percent success rate", also based on unpublished data. Moderna and the AstraZeneca Oxford collaboration will soon release their vaccine trial results. Hopefully, with full data sets and independent verification.

Warp speed

THE previous record for turning around a vaccine is four years, so 10 months is extraordinary. Pfizer partnered with Germany's BioNTech in 2018 to develop mRNA vaccines against influenza, so they hit the ground running when China released the virus genome in January, and started on a vaccine containing just part of the genetic code for the SARS-CoV-2 spike protein.

The aim was to deliver this mRNA instruction to the body's cells, so the viral spike protein is expressed on the surface and an immune response generated. By not using any live or inactivated virus, the hope was that side effects would be minimal (although there is always a chance of an immune over-reaction to the spike proteins once expressed).

The US Food and Drug Administration (FDA) granted the vaccine fast-track designation on 13 July as a leading candidate, and by 12 September it had expanded enrolment for its Phase 3 trial up to 44,000 participants in more than 120 clinical sites across the US, Brazil, South Africa and Argentina.

Interim analysis

PARTICIPANTS (43,538 of them) were recruited into a double-blind trial, with half receiving two doses of the vaccine 21 days apart, half receiving two doses of placebo, but neither researcher nor volunteer knowing which they got. Researchers waited until 94 participants had caught Covid (naturally). By then, 38,955 participants had received both doses of either placebo or vaccine. An independent committee then "unblinded" the study and found that about 90 percent of the Covid cases were in the placebo group. Equally importantly, no severe side effects were recorded in the vaccine group. The raw numbers, ages, ethnicity and severity of illness weren't released. The trial will go on until there have been 164 confirmed infections, but the glowing press release may make it harder to justify giving remaining participants a second dose of placebo. All participants must be followed up for two years.

What it means

THE preliminary results suggest the vaccine is effective at preventing the disease of Covid, but we don't yet know if it prevents infection and transmission of the SARS-CoV-2 virus, or just the progression of infection to disease. We also don't know if it prevents serious disease or death. We will only know that when the vaccine is rolled out to more people, who will have to accept this is a work in progress where we don't have all the answers.

Vaccines often work better in trials than the real world, when they are given to older people with weaker immune responses. With limited supplies, the vaccine needs to be given not just to those at risk but those in whom it works and those most likely to spread. We also don't yet know if it is safe to give the vaccine to those who have already been infected.

Should I have the vaccine?

MD will have a vaccine if it's approved by the Medicines and Healthcare products Regulatory Agency (MHRA). This is partly because I've had all my recommended MHRA approved vaccines over a lifetime, never had serious side effects and never had a disease I was protected against. But I'm also prepared to take an unknowable risk on the long-term safety of a new vaccine for my own, and the common good. I want protection from Covid and protection from passing infection on.

The trial, and the progress that results from it, would not have been possible without volunteers willing to take unknown risks on a new technology for the common good. To a lesser extent, this will also be the case when the vaccine is rolled out. Think of it as a larger trial in progress, after very encouraging early results. It should be your choice to be vaccinated, without coercion. Whether or not you have the vaccine, eating well, staying physically fit and taking a vitamin D supplement may also reduce your risks of Covid harm.

Logistics

THE potential benefits of the vaccine are huge if the "90 percent Covid prevention" figure stands up in real life. It's also good "proof of concept" news for other vaccines for Covid and many other diseases using similar technology. It could usher in more breakthroughs. The logistics are hugely complex, and if any government could screw them up, ours can. We've pre-ordered 40m doses of the Pfizer vaccine manufactured in Germany and Belgium. Its transportation is time and temperature critical. So there must be no issues that prevent free and fast movement of goods at our borders in January.

40m doses will vaccinate 20m people (currently the over 50s). The army may be called in to help. GP practices and staff will apparently offer vaccination seven days a week, with hospital staff called in to help – inevitably reducing other services. The vaccine has to be transported at -70°C and lasts for a week in a GP's fridge. So all 975 doses in a minimum-sized delivery would have to be given in a week to avoid waste.

The opportunity cost is also considerable. Research by the Health Foundation found there were 4.7m fewer people referred for routine hospital care in England between January and August 2020 compared to the same period in 2019. GPs diverted into the vaccine programme will be even less likely to get on top of this backlog, and access for routine care may become harder. Serious thought needs to be given to avoiding further non-Covid harms.

Money well spent?

THE government will be hoping the Oxford-AstraZeneca vaccine isn't far behind Pfizer. Not only is it logistically easier (kept at fridge temperature), but it'll be cheaper. Pfizer will charge nearly £30 for its two doses, plus high storage costs, whereas EU countries have been offered the Oxford vaccine for just £2.23 per dose, and the UK may get a discount as the government helped fund the research. We have pre-ordered 100m doses.

We have already trashed the economy twice, thrown £12bn (more than we spend on general practice in a year) at a test and trace system which the government's advisory group SAGE said has "marginal benefit", and we are spending £43bn on unproven mass testing. Many contracts, consultancies and leadership positions have been awarded without tendering or interview to Tory loyalists, many of whom have no expertise in the field. And our performance on nearly every measure has been one of the worst in the EU. No wonder we are banking on a vaccine.

Precautionary principle

COMPARE our predicament to countries that urgently protected their borders and controlled the virus so well that life is nearly back to normal without a vaccine, where Covid and non-Covid harms have been minimised, economies are growing and testing costs less because there is less virus to test for.

Taiwan's test spend per capita is a fraction of the UK's. A Cochrane Rapid Review of evidence looked at 12 studies on Covid-19. It found that restricting cross-border travel at the beginning of an outbreak may reduce new cases by 26 percent to 90 percent, but you have to act quickly before community transmission takes over.

Alas, we didn't act quickly to stop border entry, we stopped testing, were forced into lockdown, screwed up testing, screwed up border control again and are now in another lockdown. Meanwhile, Australia and New Zealand are playing rugby in crowded stadiums with no need for masks. As one New Zealand doctor told MD: "Your pandemic response is like your rugby. Slow, confusing, clumsy, panicky and backwards."

Vested interests

ANTI-VAXXERS have many ridiculous conspiracies: no vaccine is needed because Covid is a hoax; Bill Gates uses vaccination programmes to implant digital microchips; the virus is caused by 5G mobile phone towers; etc. But there are two accusations that need addressing.

The first is that governments, health services, health professionals and drug companies have a history of covering up medical scandals and may do so again. This is evidently true, which is why support for whistleblowers, full disclosure of data and release of trial results only after they are independently verified is vital.

The second is that "Covid-19 vaccinations are a plot by big pharma and scientists to make money". Bourla's share bonanza rather makes that point. Drug development is an incestuous world. Sir Patrick Vallance, the UK's chief scientific adviser, previously worked for the drug company GSK and holds shares. He could profit from any GSK vaccine success, but the government view is that this is not a conflict of interest since he is not involved in commercial decisions regarding vaccines.

Many of those on the SAGE committees will have been in paid

or unpaid advisory roles in drug or vaccine development, or received research funding from drug companies, charities with drug company links or government to develop vaccines. Potential conflicts of interest are everywhere in healthcare. They need to be openly declared.

What the vaccine won't fix

VACCINES aren't the only answer. An effective test, trace, isolate and support system is vital to break chains of transmission, but we still don't have this more than nine months after the first known UK infection.

---

4 November: MPs vote 516–39 to support four-week lockdown for England that comes into force next day. **5 Nov**: UK Statistics Authority criticises government's presentation of data to justify the lockdown. Furlough scheme further extended to end of March. **9 Nov**: Trials suggest Pfizer/BioNTech vaccine protects 90 percent of recipients. **11 Nov**: UK becomes fifth country to record 50,000 Covid-related deaths, after US, Brazil, India and Mexico. **13 Nov**: Data from Public Health England suggests people with learning difficulties are six times more likely to die from coronavirus in England. **16 Nov**: UK records 598 deaths, highest since 12 May.

MD on The UK's balancing act

Private Eye 1536   Press day: 30 November

14,408 daily cases   **441** daily deaths   **58,448** UK deaths to date

Tiers all round

IF you lose control in a pandemic (again), there is no solution that does not cause significant harm to many people. The seeds of our current situation were sown over summer, when we let the virus simmer rather than suppress it. Testing, tracing, isolating, spacing and quarantining were all substandard. We then turbocharged spread by combining holiday return with Eat Out to Help Out and sent workers, students and pupils off to spread at the same time. It's no surprise we are where we are.

One of the side effects of the UK trying to keep Covid at a manageable level, rather than strictly suppressing it, is that levels go up and down like a yo-yo, often very quickly due to exponential growth followed by brutal isolation. Hence the endless dispiriting cycle of restrict and release: national lockdown, regional tiers, freedom… and repeat until a vaccine arrives.

England's latest tiers were decided before debate in the Commons and in many cases without consulting local authorities. Public and political endorsement will depend on the evidence. Those in Tier 3 boroughs with lower rates than many in Tier 2 will be hardest to assuage. MD is in Tier 2 (North East Somerset), but two miles from Tier 3 (North Somerset), so expecting some cross-border pub raids. Hopefully the review on 16 December will be more logical and democratic. The aim is to keep numbers falling before festivities kick in. Many citizens weren't able to visit others for Easter, Passover, Eid, Rosh Hashana or Diwali. But we can all have a three-household, five-day Christmas.

Christmas baubles

THE three-household Christmas bubble is likely to be wilfully and mistakenly misinterpreted. Some will just read the headline and assume they can meet up as three different households every day for five days.

And a household can range from one to ten people or more.

In essence, individuals and families are being left to decide their own risks, just as we do in the flu season (although Covid is far more lethal than most flu seasons). If you want to reduce the risks, eat outdoors or with the windows open. If nothing else, it reduces the side effects of sprouts.

Family fortunes

MANY people judge their Covid risk according to their experience of it, rather than the statistics or the government's advice. MD has had three family members knowingly infected thus far, one of whom made a rapid and complete recovery, another who has disabling long Covid, and a third who died, having contracted Covid in hospital.

At a sprightly 85, he tripped and broke his hip, had very successful surgery but picked up the virus on the rehabilitation ward and died very quickly. A decent death at 85; but he could well have lived another five years without his hospital-acquired infection, reminiscent of the dark days of MRSA, when the NHS would spend a fortune on high-tech surgery only for patients to die of infection on the post-operative ward. A significant percentage of Covid infection is still being acquired in hospitals, which is why targeted testing of NHS and care home staff and visitors is essential.

Targeted testing

TESTING can make a big dent in a pandemic, but only if people get results quickly, contacts are traced and supported, and people act appropriately. Countries that managed to suppress the virus had early testing capacity, quick turnaround and relentlessly targeted the pre- and post-exposure contacts of known cases, isolating super-spreaders and breaking chains of transmission. Having suppressed the virus, they now spend a tiny fraction of what the UK does on testing.

Outsourced T&T in the UK has failed to reach millions of contacts, and currently misses 40 percent. It's due another £7bn on top of the £12bn it's already swallowed, for "marginal gains", according to SAGE.

Mass testing

T&T currently has no hope of reaching enough contacts to stem the tide, so the government is pinning its hopes (and £43bn-£100bn) on mass testing whole populations in Tier 3 regions, and students returning for Christmas, using new lateral flow tests that give results in 30 minutes. This is a screening programme whose benefits and risks should have the approval of the NHS National Screening Committee (they don't). It's also monumentally expensive, and the money might be better spent investing in public services or fixing targeted T&T. And also: will it work?

Lateral thinking

THE government claims that rapid lateral flow tests are "accurate and sensitive enough to be used in the community". But are they? How likely is it that students with two negative lateral flow tests will be free from SARS-CoV-2 when they go home for Christmas?

An analysis by PHE Porton Down and Oxford University of the Innova test the UK is using found an alarmingly high false negative rate (ie testing negative when you are in fact positive). Accuracy also depends on who does the test. When scientists do it, the test has a 20.8 percent false negative rate. When trained healthcare workers do it, it's 27 percent. When people self-test, it's 42.5 percent. So a significant number of students who test themselves negative twice will still be carrying the virus and could infect those at home.

Some universities are being honest about this uncertainty; others are offering false reassurance that negative means negative. But not all positives mean positive either. As Birmingham biostatistics professor John Deeks says: "In a population of 100,000 where 400 are infected, the test would show 630 infections, but with just 230 of those actually positive." So it misses 170 true positives and labels 400 people as positive when they're not, forcing them and their contacts to wrongly self-isolate. He concludes: "The test is thus entirely unsuitable for the government's claim that it will allow the safe 'test and release' of people from lockdown and students from university." Let's hope more accurate tests arrive soon.

Error count

"THE more certain someone is about Covid-19, the less you should trust them." So declared George Davey Smith, a professor in clinical epidemiology, in the *British Medical Journal* (19 October). Davey Smith and the *BMJ* organised a conference on "Uncertainty in a Pandemic", with more than 30 global experts invited to admit what they'd got wrong. MD was MC.

My biggest error was thinking SARS-CoV-2 would behave like SARS-Cov-1 in 2003, and so could be stopped before becoming a pandemic. Many experts also thought it would largely remain in Asia. One thought it would be no more harmful than flu. Davey Smith predicted that children would amplify the spread of SARS-CoV-2 and lead to substantial mortality in others. They haven't. Other experts predicted that widespread undocumented transmission would mean a large proportion of the UK population was infected during the first wave. It wasn't. Another thought Covid deaths would be restricted to 20,000 in the UK. Some thought that countries hit hardest in the spring would escape from being hardest hit in the autumn. Wrong again.

In New Zealand, they realised initial talk of containment was the wrong approach for them and went all out for suppression. Some talked about the error of not even trying to model the non-Covid harms of lockdown so we may never know if our approach has done more good than harm. And some cited the error of introducing interventions without proper evaluation (public masks, test and trace, mass testing, tiered lockdowns, mass lockdowns, etc) so we many never know what works best.

Speedy vaccines

NO expert predicted how effective vaccines would appear to be, at least from the press releases. There was joy and relief at the extraordinary achievements of scientists and trial volunteers in accelerating a process that used to take ten years to ten months, tempered with caution that all the data needed to be peer-reviewed and published rather than PR'd.

There is now a huge burden of responsibility on regulators such as the UK's MHRA. This is the first time in history we will have multiple vaccines for the same disease. There will be vaccines the state has bought on your behalf and (eventually) vaccines you can buy privately.

With so many vaccines in play, data monitoring of safety and effectiveness in the real world will have to be exemplary. Many drug companies have passed liability for any unforeseen vaccine harms on to governments, as part of pre-agreed deals. And governments will vary widely in what compensation they offer in the rare instances of severe side effects. No one knows for how long vaccines will give protection or how often they will have to be modified as the virus mutates, but manufacturers will make a lot more money if it becomes an annual vaccination.

Cost-price convenience

THE Oxford University-AstraZeneca (OAZ) collaboration is not only pricing at cost ($3 a dose maximum) for rich countries until at least July 2021, but will sell at cost to developing countries in perpetuity. Johnson & Johnson has also promised vaccines at cost. The OAZ vaccine can be stored for long periods in an ordinary refrigerator, from 2-8°C, which makes it much easier to use in the developing world than the Pfizer vaccine ($15 a dose).

Pfizer's share price soared when it announced its results ("90 percent effective"), as did Moderna's ("95 percent effective"). However, AstraZeneca's share price has fallen after a confusing press release stated it was "70-90 percent effective, depending on the dosage regimen". A small cohort of younger patients were given an initial half dose in error, which proved more effective than two full doses. This may be because a full first dose causes a bigger response to the viral vector (a weakened chimpanzee adenovirus) than the SARS spike protein. OAZ is now doing a further trial in elderly patients to see if this serendipitous discovery applies to them too.

Aussie rules

AUSTRALIA is the island nation most culturally similar to the UK. It has opted for strict virus suppression rather than a rollercoaster of containment like us. So should we, and can we still, do likewise?

MD is a dual national and has relatives in Australia, none of whom has knowingly been infected or knows anyone who has been. Australia is less densely populated than the UK, with far fewer travel routes, but it is also more authoritarian (voting is compulsory) and enjoys more public compliance. It chose to sacrifice international and inter-state travel and tourism to suppress the virus as much as possible, and to protect the rest of its economy. It had a recent large outbreak in Melbourne, which it suppressed very strictly and effectively, despite some protests and some people being held in chokeholds by security guards and police for not wearing masks in shops. There have been zero cases in Victoria for 30 days.

A relative of mine was allowed to fly from Brisbane to Perth for a friend's funeral, only for permission to be revoked after she had checked in her baggage. International border control in Australia is probably beyond anything the UK public would tolerate.

The price of suppression

ENTRY to Australia has been restricted since March, with borders closed except for Australian citizens, permanent residents or those with (rare) exemptions. Even if you have a home to go to, you are escorted from the airport by police to a hotel chosen for you, where you stay for 14 days without leaving the room. Regular health and attendance checks are made, with heavy fines for miscreants, and all meals are booked online and delivered.

The cost of quarantine is around A$3,000 (£1,650), which you pay for. Repayment options are available. After serving your time and paying up, you're given a wrist band. The vast majority comply with quarantine.

Go compare

IN the UK, we let 20m passengers in at the start of the pandemic with no border measures. We now have 14-day quarantine from select countries, which can occur at home or in a hotel. Compliance has been very poor (11 percent, says one study) and poorly enforced, and there is now uproar at the thought of paying for a (possibly inaccurate) lateral flow test to release you after five days.

Australian citizens need an exemption to leave Australia unless ordinarily resident elsewhere, although they can travel to New Zealand. They have far less protection for cancelled international holidays than the UK, and the travel and tourism industry – reeling from the 2020 bushfires – has taken another huge hit.

But travel and tourism in the UK have also taken a huge hit because people don't want to visit a country where the virus is out of control. In Australia, inter-state borders are reopening, sports stadia are filling up and economic harms, health harms and unemployment figures are likely to be lower than in the UK. [*Note: In fact the cost to the Australian economy is now estimated at A$311bn (£169.8bn), compared to the UK's current pandemic spend of £372bn.*] You can visit your rellies in care homes, and have Christmas together without infecting them. The lesson is clear. It was never a choice between protecting citizens from Covid or protecting them from economic harm: you have to prevent Covid to prevent economic harm.

---

19 November: OAZ vaccine reported to show strong immune response in people in their 60s and 70s. **20 Nov**: Matt Hancock says Pfizer/BioNTech vaccine could be rolled out from next month. **23 Nov**: Government hopes to inoculate all most at risk by Easter. PM details "winter plan": families can bubble in three-household groups from 23-27 December. **26 Nov**: New tier system announced for England from 2 Dec; large parts of Midlands, North-east and North-west to be Tier 3. **27 Nov**: Hospitals in England told to prepare for vaccine rollout in ten days. **28 Nov**: Nadhim Zahawi appointed minister in charge of rollout. **30 Nov**: Trials show Moderna vaccine highly effective.

"Tier 3... and you?"

MD's Nine lessons from Covid

Private Eye 1537   Press day: 14 December

22,983 daily cases   **424** daily deaths   **64,402** UK deaths to date

1. Celebrate science

WHATEVER your view on the profits of the pharmaceutical industry, the extraordinary achievement in producing Covid vaccines within a year deserves praise. Not only could vaccines save lives and prevent transmission, they could also return life to a semblance of normality. Even countries with far better control of the virus than us will embrace vaccination, though they have bought more time to ponder which vaccine they want to use.

The UK is not in that position. Having failed to act quickly at the start of the pandemic, and with widespread community transmission only partly curtailed by harmful restrictions, we are acting most quickly with vaccinations. If they work, and enough people choose to be vaccinated, it's the UK's best chance of ending lockdowns, protecting the NHS and care homes, reopening society and boosting employment and the economy.

Indirectly, vaccination could make it easier for non-Covid conditions to be diagnosed and treated, improve mental and sexual health, end isolation and allow people to die and grieve with support and dignity. But mass vaccination won't happen overnight. And it isn't harmless.

2. First do the least harm. Then do some good

"FIRST do no harm" is my least favourite aphorism. In truth, every health intervention can do harm as well as good. Merely labelling someone with high blood pressure or high Covid risk can have profound psychological consequences.

This pandemic has taught us that "do no harm" is for the birds. Every public health intervention made in the name of containing Covid – isolation at the end of life; banning funerals; banning social gatherings; closing schools, businesses and sports, hospitality and cultural venues; protecting the NHS at the cost of care homes; national lockdown, regional lockdown; failures of testing, tracing and PPE, and so on – has had significant costs and harms.

Because we were late to act at the start and let the virus run free, we have spent a staggering £280bn trying to slow it down. But we can never be sure how many lives have been saved by locking down or how many we would have saved by spending the money on other things, or more effectively. We may never know if we've done more good than harm, but we do know the harm we have inflicted on ourselves is so big you can see it from space. In such a festival of self-harm, not having a vaccine because no one can guarantee it is "100 percent safe" or "completely free from harm" seems odd, particularly when you consider the potential good it could do.

3. There is no 'zero risk'

NOTHING in a pandemic has a better benefit:risk ratio than vaccines. When rare but serious side effects occur, such as severe allergy and anaphylaxis, they happen at the time of administration, which is why vaccines are given where resuscitation is available. Of the thousands of Pfizer BioNTech vaccines given in the UK so far, two people have had severe allergic reactions and recovered with treatment. Both had a history of severe allergy to triggers other than vaccines, and anyone with such a history should not have the Pfizer vaccine.

When vaccines are given to billions of people, as they will be for Covid, thousands of adverse reactions will be reported. Most will be unrelated to the vaccines, but some will be. This is why vaccination should be voluntary and all vaccines should be protected by the Vaccine Damage Payment Scheme.

4. Keep vaccines voluntary

IN MD's view, forcing people to have vaccines against their will does more harm than good, and may increase side effects (if you think something is going to harm or help you, often it does). Some people may refuse inoculation because of a TikTok celebrity who will happily snort cocaine imported in a mule's rectum but tell his millions of followers a rigorously tested vaccine is dangerously impure.

In the dark days of medical paternalism, patients were told their tests, jabs, treatment or screening were a "jolly good idea" by a doctor or nurse they had no choice but to trust. There was little nuanced discussion about the pros and cons. Many patients are still happy to do whatever the doctor/nurse/NHS/Queen recommends, particularly in a crisis. But others want proper informed consent. The government and NHS need to give it to them.

5. Brains need BRAUNS

INFORMED choice for any medical intervention requires BRAUNS. You need to know and understand the Benefits, Risks, Alternatives, Unknowns, what if I did Nothing?, and Safety net if something goes wrong.

The NHS does not have a glorious history in giving fully informed consent for mass screening, mass vaccination or indeed any new product (eg the vaginal mesh), and regulators don't always protect people when shit happens (read *First Do No Harm*, the coruscating Independent Medicines and Medical Devices Safety Review chaired by Baroness Cumberlege).

The Pfizer Covid vaccine uses a new technology and the trial safety data and efficacy (available at *www.gov.uk*) are excellent. However, you never know how a new vaccine (or any therapy) will perform and how long protection will last until you try it in the real world. No severe allergic reactions were reported in the trials, but they happen in real life.

The chances of having short or long-term serious side effects for existing vaccines is roughly one in 25,000. The chances of having life-threatening side effects is roughly one in 1,000,000. This compares to one in 250 and one in 10,000 for a course of antibiotics, making vaccines roughly 100 times safer to take than, say, penicillin. And much less harmful than lockdown.

6. Scepticism can be healthy and harmful

THOSE who do not wish to be vaccinated should have that choice respected. However, they should also be made aware of the potential dangers of not vaccinating, to others as much as themselves. We have a long-established, safe and highly effective MMR vaccine. Unfortunately, too many parents still doubt it decades after the Andrew Wakefield autism scare, and the UK has now lost its measles-free status. The *Eye* got MMR wrong and was corrected by MD (see *Eyes passim*).

It is very hard to prove a drug or vaccine is safe and effective (trials have to be large and meticulously conducted). It is also very hard to disprove an allegation of harm, however implausible. Vaccines have done far more good than harm over centuries, but some – or some batches – have been harmful and needed to be called out. We shouldn't put a halo around any intervention, but neither should we smear it with bullshit. Transparency over data and safety reporting is key. The pharma industry has been too slow to put all data for all trials in the public domain, but Covid vaccines are likely to be the most scrutinised in history.

Herd immunity will require a majority of eligible Brits to be vaccinated. It will also need huge levels of public trust (undermined by the misinformation of the Brexit debate) and a strong sense of the importance of the collective over the individual (not a traditional selling point of the hard Tory right). It may take the Queen and David Attenborough to get it over the line.

7. Promote health for all

VACCINES save millions of lives, but not as many as giving everyone a decent standard of living. The most reliable indicator of health is wealth. Money buys freedom, space, nutritious food, care and escape from adversity, which translates in the UK to ten years more life expectancy and 20 more years of disease-free living compared to the poorest.

The pandemic, and our response to it, has magnified existing health inequalities. During the first wave it doubled your risk of death, and during the current wave it's adding 20 percent. So the more at risk you are by dint of age, disease, disability or deprivation, the more likely you are to die during the pandemic (and not necessarily of Covid).

Countries with the highest death tolls were not only poorly prepared and slow to react, but also had very high levels of health inequality, poverty, mental illness, obesity and chronic disease. For example, the "Northern Powerhouse" area has suffered 12 more Covid-related deaths per 100,000 than the rest of England and will also be hardest hit by lockdowns, recession and Brexit. Time to level up.

8. Health workers are human not heroes

MOST NHS staff enjoyed the Thursday clapping and rainbows, but many (including MD) were uncomfortable with the "heroes" label. To do a very stressful job competently, in the most difficult circumstances, we need adequate training, supervision, sleep, nutritious food, regular breaks and freedom from fear and bullying. We also need adequate PPE to protect us. The idea that we have heroic stamina and invincibility is dangerous nonsense.

Hospital-acquired Covid infections are at an all-time high (on 6 December, they accounted for 24 percent of the total), and 36 trusts saw Covid admissions increase by more than 20 percent with 19 days still to go before Christmas. True, winter is always tough in the NHS (four years ago, the Red Cross described the trolley queues in our emergency departments as a "humanitarian crisis"), but 25 percent of junior doctors in many hospitals (including my own) are currently off sick or isolating as Covid contacts. Some staff over 50 are very unwell with Covid, 650 health and care staff died from Covid this year and 2020 has also been a terrible year for mental health. Many doctors are innately self-critical workaholics who hate not being able to deliver a decent standard of care for all their patients. Please think of that when you're complaining how hard it is to see a consultant or GP. We have no heroic power to fix an overloaded system.

There is light at the end of the tunnel, but the tunnel is longer than you think and Christmas will be particularly treacherous. Think carefully before embracing the multi-household bubble-fest. My mum (84) has chosen to have the vaccine but not to have Christmas with her grandchildren.

9. How we die matters

HUMANS are the one species who know our fate well in advance, and our mortality rate will always be 100 percent. It's how we die that matters. Some people were taken well before their time by Covid, but the median age of Covid death is 82.4 years.

The greatest trauma is that many people died quickly and unexpectedly, often on their own and without a chance to say goodbye. Funerals have been strictly spaced and limited, leading to even more isolation and grief. Most people would choose a quick death over weeks of wasting away, but for those left behind the loss is more profound if words are left unsaid.

Of the many cultural shifts of the pandemic (face-masks, elbow bumps, Jonathan Van-Tam action dolls), the least understood is the extraordinary increase (more than 25,000) in people dying at home. Few had Covid tests, and postmortems have been limited, so we may never know why. Some may have lived if they'd sought help for, say, a heart attack or cancer. Many may have been fearful of catching Covid in hospital without realising they'd already caught it. Some may have wanted to "protect the NHS" when they most needed to use it. There may even be a link between "working from home" and "dying at home".

Hopefully, some people had decent deaths at home, surrounded by the love of their family, rather than saying goodbye in a mask and visor at two metres or via an iPad. Vaccines could end this insanity too. I'll be having mine. Merry Christmas.

---

1 December: BioNTech/Pfizer and Moderna file for EU vaccine approval. **2 Dec:** European Medicines Agency criticises UK decision to approve Pfizer vaccine so quickly. **5 Dec:** Matt Hancock says a vaccine could lead to looser restrictions by March. **8 Dec:** UK administers first dose of Pfizer vaccine. **10 Dec:** London sees 191.8 cases per 100,000 people per week – highest rate in England. **12 Dec:** Scientific experts urge people to rethink Christmas plans and warn the country is heading towards "disaster". **14 Dec:** Matt Hancock says a new variant of the virus has been identified and is spreading faster in some areas. The WHO says Santa Claus is immune to coronavirus.

*"First, a look at the deaths
for Christmas week..."*

MD on An evolving crisis

Private Eye 1538   Press day: 4 January 2021
57,234 daily cases   **714** daily deaths   **75,475** UK deaths to date

The front line

THE benefits of vaccinating frontline NHS staff early are multiple. You protect them, you hopefully stop them passing the virus on, and you keep them at work to keep both Covid and non-Covid services running. Hospitals now have record numbers of Covid patients, but they have far more staff off sick or isolating. Those still at work are very tired and very angry that we have sleepwalked into another entirely predictable surge.

The NHS often struggles to provide the basics for staff (safe staffing levels, space to sleep and relax, nutritious food, functioning IT). At the very least, vaccinating staff as a priority would reassure them we value them enough to protect them. The same argument applies to other key workers at risk: teaching staff; police officers; transport workers; retail workers; cleaners; delivery drivers; etc. Anyone at higher risk of infection and transmission because of their essential occupation should be vaccinated ASAP.

Seasoned adversary

MUCH is still unknown about how this pandemic will play out, but from the outset two predictions were likely to come true: 1) We would need vaccines to outfox the virus; and 2) The times of highest risk for further waves would be the autumn return to school, university and work. And winter.

The good news is that we now have two vaccines approved by the UK's MHRA. If we stay afloat until spring – physically, mentally and economically – the purgatory could finally end. The bad news is that the winter surge is as bad as we could have predicted, and we are again behind the curve.

Pandemic rules

THE first rule of pandemics is tough: there is no option that won't cause significant harm. The second rule sounds simple: the sooner you act, the less the harm, both from the virus and the measures put in to control it. But no politician likes causing significant harm, even if it prevents greater harm. So over-optimistic dithering is too often the norm.

Home secretary Priti Patel claims the government has been "consistently ahead of the curve in its response to the coronavirus". The evidence suggests otherwise. There is a subtle but important difference between acting fast to prevent a crisis and acting fast having precipitated a crisis through inaction.

Two schools

TWO schools of thought emerged at the start of the pandemic: a) Do whatever it takes to suppress the virus to an absolute minimum; and b) Contain the virus at a reproductive rate less than 1. Had we known in March 2020 that we would have vaccines in December, it would have been easier to sell suppression. It requires harsher measures earlier, but once the numbers are low they are much easier to keep there with test and trace. Containment measures are less harsh but there is much less margin of error. Miss a surge and you get caught out by exponential growth, test and trace can't cope and you end up in harsh measures anyway but with far more deaths. We're here for the third time now.

Made in the UK

MANY other countries are struggling to contain winter waves but, as in spring and autumn, our current outbreak is one of the largest. Variant strains are most likely to thrive in countries that have long-standing poor control and plenty of opportunity for natural selection (eg the UK and South Africa). The advantage of being an island is that you can control your borders to keep the virus out. But if you nurture a new variant, other countries can control their borders to keep *you* out. Alas, for many of the 40 countries that promptly isolated the UK, the variant had probably already arrived.

Hello, B.1.1.7, aka VUI 202012/01

UK SCIENCE is very good at spotting and sequencing new strains, if not naming them. The variant under investigation (VUI) first emerged in September and has spent months competing for dominance. It appears to have a transmission rate that is 71 percent higher than other variants, so no wonder it has been selected to thrive. It may also pack a higher viral load, be harder to test for and be more transmissible by children. On the upside, the vaccines should still work. Even if we hadn't spotted this new variant, it was clear from rising hospital admissions in early December that we had a big problem.

Winter woe

THE NHS is always overloaded in winter, not least from the consequence of respiratory viruses. We now have more hospital admissions with Covid than we did at the spring peak, with the effects of Christmas mixing yet to be felt. Our treatment has improved, but that also means people are staying in hospital longer, in wards and units that are more spaced out. On 29 December, 23 hospital trusts had more than a third of their beds occupied by Covid-19 patients, and occupancy was rising across the UK. Our safety net for just this moment was to spend £220m on Nightingale hospitals with more than 10,000 beds to relieve the pressure. Alas, we can't staff them and they have been barely used.

Christmas message

WITH admissions rising in early December, we could have used the good news of imminent vaccines to tighten restrictions further, move Christmas to July, postpone non-essential pleasures and reduce the obvious risk of mixing indoors. When the vaccines kick in, there will be a massive rebound in fortunes and goodwill for the tourism, travel, art, retail, entertainment and hospitality sectors. They should be supported to survive until the spring. We are delaying gratification, not ending it entirely. Most people would have understood that message. Instead, we relaxed and carried on mixing. Boris Johnson even declared it would be "inhuman" to cancel his five-day, three-household Christmas spread-fest, days before a sudden U-turn. It was a gift for the virus.

Mutant on the loose

IF YOU want people to panic in a pandemic, the word "mutant" is up there with "zombie" and "flesh-eating". Tell people a mutant strain of Covid is rampaging through London and the South-east, as health secretary Matt Hancock and Johnson did to justify their last-minute reversal, and they're as likely to pack like sardines on to the last train out of St Pancras as to isolate sensibly indoors, so increasing spread across the UK rather than reducing it. Cries from Hancock that this was "grossly irresponsible" had little effect given his prior support for Dominic Cummings.

With citizens fleeing the mutant and many countries isolating from us, we tried a linguistic downgrade from "mutant" to "variant". But the spreading was done and we'd labelled ourselves Plague Island to boot, at precisely the time we were selling ourselves to the world as a free nation. Come trade and plague with us!

Personal responsibility

MANY people gave up listening to Johnson on matters pandemic when he nearly died after a round of hospital handshakes. Many had decided to cancel Christmas, or curtail it, long before his 11th-hour reverse ferret. Many have followed the rules religiously throughout. And some have still ended up in hospital with Covid. Others have caught Covid in hospital.

Irrespective of the competence of our political leadership, a virus that spreads quickly and silently can only be slowed if enough of us stick to the rules. We haven't. The British thirst for freedom, individualism and ignoring experts gives us great art and comedy, but dreadful infection control. We can resist everything but temptation. We will always find selfish excuses to bend or break the rules and justify our risky behaviour.

The wide variation in Covid deaths per head of different populations tells its own story. In countries of at least 20m inhabitants, deaths range from more than one in every 1,000 (UK and US) to one per 2,500 (Canada, Germany), one per 29,000 (Australia), one per 65,000 (South Korea), one per 325,000 (Kenya) and one per 3,400,000 (Taiwan). In the lowest-risk countries, a major incident is declared if a handful of cases emerges and rapid action is taken to isolate. In the UK, we tolerate tens of thousands of new cases a day. Why?

First among unequals

IF the SARS-CoV-2 virus harmed everyone equally, including children, more people would take it seriously. Some young, fit patients have suffered but the virus has predominantly harmed the elderly, the disabled, the poor and those with pre-existing conditions. Some of those at low risk argue that they should be free to go about their business while those at high risk are shielded.

The moral debate on shielding could outlast the pandemic, but it was never workable. The UK has huge numbers of people at risk of premature death or harm not just from Covid but all manner of non-contagious diseases. There are 25m people in the higher-risk vaccine categories by dint of age, disease or disability. It would be impossible to shield them all even if it were desirable.

More pertinently, the UK has tolerated these alarming health inequalities for decades. Covid has merely highlighted them. If you don't mind living in a country where the poorest die a decade younger than the richest and suffer 20 more years of chronic disease, you're probably not too fussed if the same people die from Covid or aren't able to get care for their other diseases because Covid has overwhelmed the NHS. Even after vaccination, the inequalities will remain. There is much levelling up to do.

Vaccination roll-out

WE were first to approve a vaccine, but Israel has quickly overtaken us in the roll-out. While our vaccines sat in fridges over the festive break, it managed 11.55 vaccination doses per 100 people (the UK is at 1.47). By 2 January, 41 percent of Israelis over 60 had already received their first vaccine.

The approval of the Oxford-AstraZeneca vaccine gives us grounds for optimism in the UK and across the world. It is much easier to transport and store than the Pfizer-BioNTech vaccine and will be far more affordable globally, where it will be sold at cost price in perpetuity. Thank you.

With infections rising fast, the aim in the UK is to give the most benefit to the most people in the shortest time, and the joint committee on vaccination and immunisation (JCVI) believes the best way to do this is to give most of the higher-risk individuals a single dose of either vaccine before giving anyone a second dose (up to 12 weeks later). Its view from the trial data is that a single dose will confer significant protection, although we don't yet know if it reduces transmission. The logic is sound but delaying a second dose too long could make it less effective or increase the risk of a resistant strain emerging.

It's also a disappointment for a million people who will now have their second Pfizer jab postponed, and a time-consuming pain in the arse for the staff who have to phone them. The rest of us will join a queue and be offered whatever vaccine is available at the time. I would happily have either and be grateful.

Thousands of vets, dentists and retired doctors and nurses have volunteered to vaccinate but are being held up by ludicrous bureaucratic requirements. If they make it through the paperwork, they also need to be vaccinated (especially those over 50) before putting themselves at risk. Indeed, anyone whose essential work is high-risk should be vaccinated as soon as possible.

Testing in schools

HAVING cried "MUTANT!" and while waiting to discover if the new variant spreads faster in children, the government should not be surprised that many teachers and parents would rather adopt the precautionary principle and keep schools closed. Mass testing of pupils with lateral flow tests is an unproven experiment. You should always act on a positive result (likely to be accurate) but not be reassured by a negative one. Analysis suggests they pick up only half the active infections, which is clearly better than nothing but hardly fool-proof. And you need to trace and isolate contacts, which we're still struggling with.

As one Tier 3 contact tracer told MD: "Many people who should be self-isolating don't find out until Day 7 or later. We publish 'the percentage of contacts traced' but if they're traced so late, what's the point? I spoke to someone today who'd just discovered they should have been isolating nine days earlier."

Long and short of it

IT took us 2.4bn years to evolve from single cells to the most dominant species on the planet, and yet microorganisms that evolve in our destructive wake can still outfox us. Mutations occur at random, but we create the context that allows microbes to cross species to us. We cut down forests to displace animals from their natural habitats, and we transport, rear and slaughter them inhumanely. We are ultimately responsible for our predicament. But whatever tier we're in, we can still read, nap, watch, walk, talk, taste, hope and help those who are really struggling. The darling buds of May aren't far away. Homely New Year.

---

19 Dec: Data suggests "Kent variant" could be 70 percent more transmissible than previous virus strains. Government restricts relaxation of festive rules to just Christmas Day. Much of London and South-east put in new Tier 4, where rules will not be relaxed. Scotland imposes travel ban with rest of UK. Total number of cases globally passes 75m. **21 Dec**: Number of people in UK who have received first vaccine dose hits 500,000. **22 Dec**: AstraZeneca says it believes its vaccine should be effective against new strain. **23 Dec**: Government says more areas of England will move into Tier 4 from Boxing Day. **25 Dec**: Queen praises Britons for "rising magnificently to the challenges of the year". Another 570 deaths are recorded, taking UK death toll over 70,000. **28 Dec**: UK reports more than 40,000 cases in 24 hours for first time. **29 Dec**: UK records more than 50,000 infections in 24 hours for first time. **30 Dec**: OAZ vaccine approved for UK use. **31 Dec**: Brazil detects two cases of Kent variant. **4 January 2021**: PM announces England's third national lockdown, to last at least six weeks from 5 January. Scotland enters lockdown. UK becomes first country to administer OAZ vaccine.

MD on Vaccinating for victory

Private Eye 1539   Press day: 18 January
40,485 daily cases   **1,224** daily deaths   **89,860** UK deaths to date

Good news, bad news

THE good news is that we are pre-testing and quarantining everyone at our borders to keep the virus and its variants out. The bad news is that it has taken the government nearly a year and 100,000 deaths to cotton on.

We are, however, leading the pack on vaccine roll-out, with 14.9m of our highest-risk citizens promised a first jab by 15 February, and a further 17m by spring. It's a tough ask, and government promises have depreciated markedly in value over the past year; but NHS GPs and pharmacies have a good track record delivering vaccines, and the addition of hospital centres and regional mega-hubs could make this achievable, provided supply can keep up with demand.

Don't have a post-vaccine party, however. Protection takes at least three weeks to kick in. We don't yet know if vaccines prevent transmission or infection, or just reduce severe infections and death. We don't yet know if the 400,000 people who have had two doses will have significantly better protection than the 4m who have had one. With the over-80s at least partially protected, Covid deaths should fall from next month, but the median age of an ITU patient is 58, so hospitals will still be busy.

To control Covid globally, all countries need fair access to vaccines. Many rich countries, including the UK, have over-ordered vaccines and must redistribute any surplus through the COVAX scheme. With more than 2m global deaths and counting, vaccination should happen according to risk, not wealth.

Despite the achievement of vaccine rollout, the UK is also leading Europe in both Covid deaths and excess deaths. Over the year, Scotland and Northern Ireland have performed better than England and Wales. Excess deaths are the best measure of how a country has dealt with the pandemic overall. It encompasses not just how well we managed to control infection and treat Covid, but how well we have promoted public health and kept other services open.

Unsurprisingly, countries with the lowest excess deaths have also suffered the least economic, educational and psychological harm. Alas, last year's deaths were up 15 percent, or 75,925 above the five-year average in England and Wales. This was the largest increase in deaths in a single year since 1940; and our life expectancy, which had levelled off alarmingly in the years preceding the pandemic, will now fall. The virus has exploited all our systemic weaknesses. We were poorly prepared for the pandemic, with poor public health and poor public service capacity; and the government played "chicken" three times with the virus on the rise, and lost.

The new variant was spreading well before Christmas, and it's impossible to know how much extra spread occurred with the "escape the mutant" rush from London and the South-east on 19 December. Many people had already planned to cut back at Christmas, but Boris Johnson "battling the experts to save Christmas" (as the *Express* put it) before making a screeching U-turn just sowed panic and confusion.

The Covid dirty bomb detonates in those most susceptible 21 days or more after infection. Whole families have gone down with the new variant and daily deaths are now higher than they ever have been. It has been clear since last March that winter would be the time of highest risk for a respiratory virus resurgence, variant or not.

An NHS overloaded with Covid now has a waiting list of 4.5m and more than 1,000 patients in London need urgent cancer surgery but have no date for it. The private sector must help. At the same time we're trying to vaccinate during an outbreak, which gives the virus more chances to spread and become resistant. So, not ideal.

Vaccinating during a surge

IT's much safer to vaccinate in advance of an outbreak, as we do with flu, than during one. The virus currently has more opportunities to mutate and may spread in clinics, which vary in how well spaced and ventilated they are. Cathedral clinics with drafts and very high ceilings would be ideal. Health and care settings are the highest-risk places to contract Covid, and many NHS staff are over 50 and overweight. Vaccinators need vaccinating too.

Vaccine homework

ACCORDING to a YouGov poll, 80 percent of Britons are willing to have a Covid-19 vaccine, although BAME citizens may need more reassurance. There are excellent information leaflets at *www.gov.uk* on vaccine types, ingredients (no pork or beef), indications, side effects and protection. If you want to delve deeper, the Green Book is the vaccination bible for NHS workers and contains much of what we currently know about the virus and the vaccines. It is also freely available on the *www.gov.uk* website (chapter 14a). You may get more than one invitation for a vaccine (from GP, pharmacy or regional mega-hub), so only accept one. If anyone asks for money or personal details, it's a hoax.

MD's jab

I HAD my first Pfizer-BioNTech jab last week at my hospital. Thank you. I had mild side effects, which are a good sign the immune system has responded to the vaccine, but it takes a few weeks for a decent measure of protection to evolve. A few of my younger NHS colleagues have had worse headaches, arm pain, enlarged lymph glands and higher temperatures post-vaccination, especially those who have already had Covid. However, nearly all pass in 48 hours.

Post-vaccine deaths

UNSURPRISINGLY, MD is already being sent social media posts claiming the Covid vaccine has killed someone. In general, vaccines are among the safest health interventions known, with around one in a million people suffering life-threatening side effects. Most recover with prompt anaphylaxis treatment, but if you vaccinate billions globally, some will die as a result of vaccination. However, many more will die from Covid, including Covid they caught around the time of vaccination that will be blamed on the vaccine. Others will die after vaccination from something completely unrelated (dementia, say). The older you are, the more likely you are to die at any time, and we are vaccinating the oldest in our population. So expect post-vaccine deaths, nearly all of which aren't vaccine-related. There is no "zero risk", and all serious after-events should be reported via the MHRA's Yellow Card Scheme.

Tribal warfare

IN A liberal democracy people are free to believe any old bollocks. The completely deluded believe Covid doesn't exist, all the tests are false, vaccines are unnecessary and our hospitals are empty. At the other end, there are those who strongly believe in the pandemic, believe it is a consequence of the way we live on this planet and that a global cull of destructive humans for virus food is welcome evolutionary payback.

Between these extremes, both pro- and anti-lockdown factions believe in vaccines. If you're anti-lockdown, you just want all the high-risk people vaccinated to reopen society completely; if you're (usually reluctantly) pro-lockdown, you think at least 70 percent of the population need to be vaccinated and even then we may be wearing masks next Christmas.

MD is far more cautious than I was a year ago. And countries who kept coronavirus at the lowest possible level have had far fewer deaths, school closures and job losses than those who tried to keep it at "a manageable level". With exponential growth, manageable very soon becomes unmanageable, as we keep discovering. And so now has Germany.

England v Germany

COMPARING the UK to New Zealand or other smaller population nations isn't fair, although we can clearly learn from them. China managed to brutally suppress the virus by brutally suppressing its people, but that isn't the British way.

Germany is democratically, culturally and climatically similar to us. It has a larger population than the UK (83.02m v 66.65m), and we have the advantage of island status to better control our borders from viral invasion. We should have outperformed Germany over the year, but it put us to shame in round one. It's still beaten us in rounds two and three, but they have been closer. So are we getting better or has Germany got worse?

Round one

PREPARATION is key in any pandemic. If we'd matched the percentage of GDP Germany has put into healthcare just since 2000, we'd have put an extra £260bn into the NHS up to 2018. Think how much extra capacity that would have bought. Germany has the most hospital beds and ITU beds per 1,000 people in the European Union. Unlike the UK, it had testing and tracing infrastructure in place at the outset, was first to come up with a PCR test, and the country's 400 local health authorities quickly tracked, traced, isolated and supported the contacts before numbers got out of control.

Crucially, it took the pandemic seriously from the outset. Angela Merkel (scientist) declared it the country's greatest threat since the Second World War, while Boris Johnson (optimist) was shaking hands in hospital and encouraging people to carry on as normal. Unsurprisingly, it's the UK that has posted the highest excess deaths since the war. Wave one German deaths peaked at 2.78 per million people, compared with 13.88 in the UK, 13.59 in Italy, 16.87 in France and 18.57 in Spain. Germany had barely any excess deaths.

Rounds two and three

GERMANY was first again to come up with a vaccine (BioNTech), but the UK wasn't far behind this time (Oxford-AstraZeneca) and we were quicker to approve vaccines and roll them out. There has also been a convergence of behaviour as we became "habituation nations". If your individual risk from infection is low, there is a limit to how long you will make huge personal sacrifices to help those less fortunate and save your health service. In both Germany and the UK, the workers most at risk from Covid can least afford to isolate. Many are under constant pressure to go to work to put food on the table. Covid is low on their daily risk list.

Germany's citizens experienced so few deaths in wave one they relaxed over the summer, and an autumn surge emerged that even their track and trace couldn't contain. It went into "lockdown light" on 2 November, with schools and nurseries remaining open. But it hasn't worked and Germany now has 1,000 Covid deaths a day. Why?

Christmas markets were largely cancelled, but there was still a lot of festive mingling and "mulled wine to go". Some restaurants bent the rules. Merkel warned that Christmas was high-risk, but under pressure from the chief ministers of Germany's federal states, rules were relaxed. It now has four times as many infections as in the peak of spring, and 4,000 Covid patients on intensive care.

As in the UK, the more infectious variant is partly responsible.

Unlike the UK, there won't be the huge number of excess deaths in Germany because it has far more healthcare capacity.

Home or hospital?

IF you get what you think is Covid and are trying to tough it out at home, when should you call for help? NHS England has an excellent leaflet – *Important information to keep you safe while isolating at home.* Ambulance services and hospitals are overloaded in many areas, and they're encouraging people to phone 111 first. The leaflet tells you when to go to A&E or call 999. GPs may provide free home-use pulse oximeters for those most at risk. It's an emergency if your blood oxygen levels are 92 percent or less (retake your reading immediately before calling). If it's 93-94 percent, call 111.

Symptoms can worsen very quickly with Covid, and indeed any health emergency. In reality, it's bloody hard to judge how sick you are when you're also frightened, which I suspect is one reason so many have died at home. Like the government, the tendency is to hope for the best and delay taking action – never a good plan in an emergency.

---

5 January: UK cancels 2021 GCSE and A-level exams. CMO Chris Whitty says one in 50 people in the UK has coronavirus. UK records more than 60,000 cases in 24 hours. **7 Jan**: Europe passes 25m coronavirus cases. **8 Jan**: Government says health and social care staff to get vaccine priority, with most vaccinated before February. Moderna becomes third vaccine approved for use in UK. US records a record 290,000 cases in 24 hours. **9 Jan**: UK passes 3m cases; deaths pass 80,000. **11 Jan**: WHO says herd immunity will not be achieved in 2021, despite vaccine rollout. **13 Jan**: UK passes 100,000 coronavirus deaths. **14 Jan**: UK bans flights from Argentina, Brazil and Chile. **17 Jan**: Vaccination of over-70s and clinically vulnerable to begin this week. **18 Jan**: UK had world's highest death toll in week ending 17 January, with 16.3 deaths per million people. But the number of UK cases fell by a quarter over preceding week.

"Roll out the vaccine..."

MD on A year of Covid

Private Eye 1540　Press day: 1 February

21,246 daily cases　**1,018** daily deaths　**106,564** UK deaths to date

Good news for some

LOCKDOWN is reducing Covid infections and hospital admissions, at a cost to education and the economy, but we should soon see a reduction in serious illness and death thanks to the success of our vaccination programme.

Vaccine nationalism from those playing catch-up is inevitable, and we must use the excess vaccines we have ordered to help the EU and beyond. Covid needs to be controlled globally or we will continue swapping new variants in our hyper-connected world.

The UK has committed £548m to the COVAX global scheme and the Oxford-AstraZeneca vaccine will be sold to developing countries at cost in perpetuity. However, they are running far behind. As of 23 January, 39m people in rich countries had been vaccinated, compared to a total in Africa of 25 people. Yes, 25.

Not up to the task

A YEAR since our first known infection, and 105,571 deaths later, it's hard to escape the conclusion that the UK was simply not up to the task of controlling Covid without vaccines. We need a swift public inquiry so lessons can be learned before the next pandemic arrives. A key one is flexibility. We were expecting influenza and we got coronavirus. Prepare for another coronavirus and we'll likely get influenza.

When you've seen one pandemic...

PREPARING for the type of virus only gets you so far. Each one is unique. When you've seen one pandemic... you've seen one pandemic.

MD made the early error of assuming the SARS-CoV-2 virus would be similar to its 2003 cousin (SARS-CoV-1), causing a very unpleasant disease in a limited number of people that was relatively easy to spot and contain. It can indeed cause a very unpleasant disease; but in addition it evolved to spread silently – asymptomatically, pre-symptomatically and with minimal symptoms – so it was everywhere on the planet before we knew it. Although an individual's risk may be reassuringly low, the law of large numbers means that a whole population exposed to a small risk will result in a large number of deaths (more than 2.2m globally).

Vaccines v variants

MORE vaccines are coming on board but exotic viral variants are on the rise – from Brazil, South Africa and Kent – which may, or may not, spread faster, be more virulent and evade some vaccines. We must do trials to see if our gamble to ignore the manufacturer's schedule and give as many high-risk individuals as possible a single dose of vaccine provides better protection than giving half the number both doses 21 days apart. Everyone should get a second dose in 12 weeks, if supply can keep up, but we may need to change tack. No matter how many times we tweak our vaccines, the virus will do its best to outfox us. Such is the wonder of evolution…

The Red Queen

THE Red Queen hypothesis of evolution is simple: predator and prey co-evolve in an escalating cycle of complexity. If foxes run faster, rabbits are selected to run faster still, forcing foxes to run even faster. If a fox's eyesight improves, then rabbits are selected to blend better with the environment, so foxes need even better eyesight to spot them. Antibiotic and vaccine resistance are good examples. As Lewis Carroll's Red Queen explains to Alice: "It takes all the running you can do, just to keep in the same place."

Fortunately the virus doesn't need to kill us to feed on us. It exists solely to reproduce and many people peacefully co-exist with it on board, as we do with many other viruses. Death of the food source is no use to the virus, although a variant that causes more severe disease forces people into homes and hospitals where there are more opportunities to spread. So we need to ventilate the buildings as much as the patients. Stuffy, ventilation-free indoor spaces can be a Covid trap.

Thinking outside the school

THE longer we cut our education provision, the more we harm our children and our future. The WHO advises that schools should be the last to close, closures should be as brief as possible, and they should be first to open. Some children have spent just 60 days in school in the last year. Laptop provision for home schooling has improved, but too many children can't afford or access decent broadband and many parents are exhausted. Children have always been at the lowest risk from Covid and the highest risk from lockdown. Their welfare is supposed to be paramount but those under 18 are not even allowed to ask questions at the government's Covid briefings.

Lateral flow tests may quickly pick up pupils and staff with the highest viral loads, but falsely reassure those whose infections are missed. Higher risk teachers and school staff should be vaccinated. But the biggest problem may be schools themselves. Most are currently open but at 20-30 percent capacity. When they return to full capacity, classrooms will be overcrowded, and many are poorly ventilated or hermetically sealed. Alternative venues could be safer.

Inverse Covid laws

LIFE is full of risks if you're obese, old, disabled and/or poor, but even more so in a pandemic. The inverse Covid laws apply. Those most at risk from Covid are least able to escape it. Those who most need to isolate can least afford to do so. Those most likely to die are least likely to access help. If you plot a graph of poverty v Covid deaths in the UK, or indeed any deaths, it makes unedifying viewing.

We can either blame people for being sitting ducks or help them put nutritious food on the table and reduce their risk of premature disease and death. Lockdown is a blunt tool with horrible side effects, and there's a limit to how much any country can harm its young to protect the rest. But if you don't control infections with border quarantine, social distancing and a functioning test, trace, isolate and support system, there is no other option.

Preparing for the worst

AT the start of a pandemic, when you can't be sure what you're dealing with, the countries that did best adopted the precautionary principle. Those previously scarred by SARS picked up on social media warnings from Wuhan whistleblowers before they were deleted, assumed China was covering up again, took rapid pre-emptive action and largely protected their citizens and their economies from Covid. The rest of the world waited for the World Health Organization, which was being led a merry dance by the Chinese government.

Anticipating the science

FOLLOWING the science is all very well, but if you wait to assemble all the facts in an exponentially growing pandemic that started in a country that covers up, you're too late. In the UK, we could not stop the virus arriving but as soon as we knew, in early March, that it was spreading so rapidly we didn't have the testing capacity to keep track of it, we should have locked down. Instead we lied about the reasons we had stopped testing, flirted dangerously with herd immunity, dithered, U-turned, locked down late and set a pattern of poor management that cost many lives.

Global inquiry

COULD the pandemic have been prevented, or severely curtailed, at its origin? A global inquiry is under way, and most countries will wait until it reports to the World Health Assembly in May before launching their own, perhaps to pin as much pre-blame as possible on the Chinese government and the WHO.

The Independent Panel for Pandemic Preparedness and Response (IPPPR) was set up by the WHO to independently and impartially criticise anyone (including the WHO), but in diplomatic terms. It can't compel witnesses to appear, but has interviewed more than 100 frontline pandemic experts. The IPPPR's second report came out last month and declared: "The global pandemic alert system is not fit for purpose... Critical elements of the system are slow, cumbersome and indecisive. The procedures and protocols... leading up to the declaration of a public health emergency of international concern seem to come from an earlier analog era and need to be brought into the digital age... This technical updating must be accompanied by a political step-change in the willingness of countries to hold themselves accountable for taking all necessary actions as soon as an alert is issued."

Ground zero, evidence zero?

A WHO team is in Wuhan, 14 months after the outbreak, to gather evidence on the precise origin. Good luck with that. Members spent the first fortnight locked in a room in a quarantine hotel where every shred of waste has to go into a bio bag. The WHO does not have the resources for an independent investigation and relies entirely on the evidence and witnesses the Chinese authorities choose to share with them.

We many never find when and where Bat Zero met Pangolin Zero before meeting Human Zero. But we do know that cramming several species of petrified wild animal into a small crate, transporting them across continents as they shit, swap and spread virus everywhere, before being slaughtered in a crowded live market, taken home and eaten is high-risk. If we allow this to happen anywhere in the world, we all pay the price. But how do we stop it?

Chinese lessons not learned

CHINA delayed owning up to SARS in 2003, and did so again this time. It delayed admitting to the outbreak, and when it did it denied the strong likelihood of human-to-human transmission, disciplined frontline whistleblowers who said otherwise, and had to be bumped into releasing the viral genome by a brave scientist who was then disciplined. The delay clearly contravened international law and caused chaos at the WHO, which didn't want to upset its second biggest funder until there was more proof, but could sense another SARS unfolding before its eyes.

The WHO kept the risk at "moderate" – which fooled MD and many others – and delayed announcing a public health emergency until 30 January, even though Wuhan had locked down on 23 January (eight weeks after the first known infection). The best chance of preventing the pandemic was already lost.

China at least controlled its own Covid, and was commended for it by the WHO. The release of the genetic sequence of the virus allowed PCR tests and vaccines to be developed. But there's no doubt its initial cover-up cost lives. Even when doctors and nurses in Wuhan were contracting the virus – obvious proof of human-to-human transmission – they were initially forbidden from wearing masks so as not to promote panic. So much for the precautionary principle.

Speed matters

IF you have, say, a heart attack or stroke, the sooner you act the better your chances of survival. The same is true in public health emergencies, and no one knew this more than Dr Michael Ryan, executive director of the WHO's health emergencies programme and an Ebola expert.

The Press Association obtained recordings of WHO meetings in January 2020 of Dr Ryan incandescent that China was withholding information that could be the best chance of preventing global spread. The WHO issued stern warnings from 30 January, with clear instructions on how to manage the outbreak, but many countries – including the UK and the US – failed to act. On 11 March, the WHO belatedly used the call-to-arms word "pandemic". Still many countries didn't act.

At a press conference on 13 March, Dr Ryan delivered the impassioned speech the world had needed to hear in early January: "You need to be prepared and you need to react quickly. You need to go after the virus. You need to stop the chains of transmission. You need to engage with communities very deeply. Community acceptance is hugely important. You need to understand the impact on schools, security and economics. You need to be coordinated and coherent. Be fast, have no regrets – you must be the first mover. The virus will always get you if you don't move quickly.

"If you need to be right before you move, you will never win. Perfection is the enemy of the good when it comes to emergency management. Speed trumps perfection. The problem we have in society at the moment is that everyone is afraid of making a mistake; everyone is afraid of the consequence of error. But the greatest error is not to move. The greatest error is to be paralysed by the fear of failure." And, in the UK, the greatest error is to be paralysed by fear of your spartan, lockdown-sceptic backbenchers and their champions in the press.

Staff are still dying

DR Gamal Osman, a frontline BAME consultant in his 60s, died from Covid on 28 January. His brother died from Covid in September but he refused to stand down, rallying his colleagues at North Bristol NHS Trust by saying: "This isn't a time for cowards." His trust could have insisted he stood down, but many hospitals and care homes would collapse if all their high-risk staff were removed from frontline care. Frontline staff must get their second vaccine doses, and have variant-proof PPE. Dr Osman was the sole earner for his wife and seven children. Colleagues have set up a GoFundMe page to support them.

---

19 January: UK records 1,610 deaths in 24 hours –highest total yet. **24 Jan**: 77 cases of South African variant identified in UK. **26 Jan**: AstraZeneca says it will prioritise delivery of vaccines to UK over the EU, as it signed contract with UK first. **27 Jan**: UK announces compulsory hotel quarantine for arrivals from "high-risk" countries. **28 Jan**: UK trials of Novavax vaccine show it to be 89.9% efficient. **29 Jan**: EU triggers, then retracts, a Brexit clause that would have blocked vaccine exports to Northern Ireland. EU authorises OAZ vaccine for use on over-18s. Trials of Belgian single-dose Janssen vaccine, of which UK has ordered 60m doses, suggests it is 66% effective. **30 Jan**: WHO urges UK to pause vaccinations after it finishes vaccinating most vulnerable, to allow poorer countries to receive the vaccine. **31 Jan**: UK delivers nearly 600,000 vaccines in a day –highest number to date. **1 February**: PM is optimistic people will be able to have summer holidays in 2021.

MD on Tough choices

Private Eye **1541**   **Press day: 15 February**
12,084 daily cases   **551** daily deaths   **117,396** UK deaths to date

Quote of the century

"Outbreaks are inevitable, but pandemics are optional." – Larry Brilliant, the American physician and pandemic expert who helped eradicate smallpox 45 years ago

Progress report

THE UK has made impressive advances, not just in the creation, manufacture and roll-out of Covid vaccines (15m and counting), but on finding drugs to treat established disease too.

The UK Recovery Trial found the cheap steroid dexamethasone reduces mortality risk by 20 percent for those on oxygen and 35 percent for ventilated patients. The government-funded REMAP-CAP trial found that two drugs normally used to treat rheumatoid arthritis – tocilizumab and sarilumab – reduce the relative risk of death for patients entering intensive care by 24 percent. And the combination dexamethasone and tocilizumab may reduce ITU mortality by up to 40 percent.

We have improved ITU management and ventilator use, and developed early warning systems to spot Covid patients deteriorating outside ITU and at home. The use of pulse-oximeters can spot patients with dangerously low oxygen saturation even when they appear well. The NHS has made vitamin D supplements free for those at high risk of Covid, in the hope of improving general health and immunity.

Compliance with masks, hand-washing, social distancing, isolating, quarantining and lockdown rules has endured, the NHS Covid app has been downloaded 22 million times and we have the world's most expensive test and trace system. Yet despite all the effort, cost, sacrifice and progress, we have been unable to stop 120,000 people dying from Covid, nor the economic and educational carnage that has accompanied it. Might it not have been better to keep the virus out at our borders?

Keeping out the variants

MD predicted that effective vaccines might yet save Boris Johnson's career, and the Tories are indeed ahead of Labour in the polls despite the grim death toll. The variants too are a political convenience.

There is no doubt the Kent variant has done a lot of damage and needed to be suppressed. It thrived in the UK because of our poor controls, and when it took off in December – as respiratory viruses tend to – it provided a much-needed excuse for Johnson to reverse his risky three-household Christmas gathering. Alas, the last-minute "mutant on the loose" message provoked panic and some people fled London and the South-east, spreading the new variant nationwide. Others felt it was too late to change plans Johnson had recently assured them it would be "inhuman" to cancel. For five weeks from 6 January, we had more deaths most days than Australia has had in the entire pandemic. My Aussie relatives are aghast at our incompetence. Yet the variant is more likely to cop the blame than the government.

Playing the fear card

THE "fear of variants" can now be used to sanction all the strategies the government should have put in place a year ago. Strict border control, stricter testing and tracing, suppression of infection rather than letting it simmer and – hopefully – better support for the poor.

Had we done this a year ago and kept infections low, we might not be in lockdown now. Vaccination will be a big help this time around, and variant fear has spawned scary Covid adverts and is making more people stick to the rules and come forward for vaccination. It's also allowed the government to up the threats. Lie about your sneaky Algarve getaway and you could outstay a prison-full of sex offenders.

Fear factors

FEAR of Covid is inevitable, especially in a country that has handled it so badly. The virus may kill around 150,000 of our citizens by the time this outbreak ends, and many more survivors will be left with a lifetime of ill-health. Alas, fear is also very bad for mental health and immunity.

Never-ending workload stress and death exposure may lead to even more NHS and social care vacancies. Many frontline staff were not given correct PPE and a recent British Medical Association (BMA) poll found that only a third of doctors feel protected at work, leading to deep-seated anger and anxiety. No one should be exposed to a biological hazard at work without the best protection. A public inquiry must investigate.

MD works in paediatrics, hence my repeated concerns about non-Covid harms and what we are doing to our children. Traumatic stress is far more likely when children don't perceive the world they live in to be safe. The unremitting daily death tolls and graphic ITU films may help compliance with the rules, but not emotional recovery. We now have variants to worry about too.

After three lockdowns and record deaths, it will take all Johnson's communication skills to convince people that fear of variants and the virus can be switched to "it's safe to go back to school" and "it's safe to summer in Skegness". His only hope of doing so is to get infections to a very low level and keep them there with mass vaccination and much-improved test and trace. In time, a less virulent variant may ride to the rescue.

Variants happen

VARIANTS are not new. As MD pointed out last March, the virus is "merrily mutating" and exists only to spread and reproduce. Our capacity for genomic sequencing is extraordinary, and we have already spotted more than 4,000 variants. The trick is to stop those selected to dominate, as they are more infectious or vaccine-resistant.

Variation may work in our favour, if the dominant strain becomes no more virulent than seasonal flu (the current strains are five to ten times more deadly). We could then live with it as we live with flu, vaccinating the most vulnerable and those most likely to spread infection each year, but never eradicating it. Or it may be that the challenge of vaccine evasion leads to more virulent variants that need to be quickly detected and suppressed. Either way, we will be heavily reliant on a properly functioning test and trace system.

For now, expect lots of small, scary variant sequencing and vaccine studies to pop up all over the world. What you need to know is that the vaccines currently available in the UK appear effective against the variants currently dominant here, and if the variants change, the vaccines can be tweaked.

My advice is to get your vaccination as soon as it's offered. You may get side effects, but nearly all go in 24-48 hours, and a single jab appears to provide good protection against severe disease and death three weeks later. You may still get a milder infection, but that's much better than hospitalisation. The *gov.uk* and NHS websites have information on vaccine trials, types and contents, and what to do and expect after vaccination.

When will lockdown end?

THE PM has two choices. The riskier one is to end lockdown when everyone in the highest risk categories has been offered a vaccine, with a few weeks to pass for the effects to kick in. The cautious one is to do the above *and* wait until infections are at a level that test and trace can properly control – say, 1,500 a day – which gives the best chance of preventing future variant waves. Teachers, parents and pupils also need to be convinced schools are safe from 8 March.

Testing will be crucial, but there is only any point if you act on the results, which means supporting people to isolate. Indeed, it is not ethical to test people without supporting them to do the right thing. Infections have always been highest in areas where people can least afford to lock down, so the expertise of local authority and NHS staff will be essential to find contacts and help them with advice and financial support. Technology can help – we can do backwards and forwards contact tracing with genomic sequencing of every positive

Chris Whitty and Patrick Vallance, the Early Years

"Next slide, please"

case. But trust in those delivering the service matters, and public servants are generally more trusted than Serco and Sitel temps.

As MD noted at the start of the pandemic: "If you don't measure, you can't manage. And you can't fight a virus if you don't know where it is." Both rapid lateral flow tests and slower PCR tests have a role, but all new tests need to be properly evaluated rather than just rolled out. And before we launch into hideously expensive mass "moonshot" testing of everyone, with its attendant false results, we need to fix the basics of breaking the chains of transmission from people who actually have symptoms. Tests should be easily available to anyone with a new runny or blocked nose, sore throat, hoarseness, muscle pains, fatigue and headache, in addition to cough, high temperature and changes in taste and smell.

Pandemic reform

IS a pandemic the right time, and excuse, to reorganise the English health service again? The government already announced the abolition of Public Health England (PHE) last August, when it hoped the pandemic was over, to be replaced by a National Institute for Health Protection, to stop future pandemics. Noted pandemic prevention expert Dido Harding was installed as "interim executive chair", as if she didn't have enough to do trying to sort out NHS Test and Trace.

This gave a clear signal that the over-centralised PHE (a Tory creation) was most to blame for pandemic failures, and not politicians or Harding. Whether the overloading of Harding or the destabilisation and demoralisation of 5,500 PHE staff played a role in the ensuing poor management is hard to judge, but it can hardly have helped. So why is the government proposing further reform of the NHS, the one part of the pandemic response that has shone?

Long time coming

THESE reforms have been coming since the Tories realised their Health and Social Care Act 2012 was a disaster, but they needed pandemic cover to ditch it. Health secretary at the time Andrew Lansley was repeatedly warned (including by MD on the BBC's *Question Time*) that feeding the NHS even more to the market would splinter it and patients would fall through the cracks between hospitals, GP practices, community services, social care and public health services. Ten years of austerity hardly helped.

Before the pandemic, NHS waiting lists and health and care staff vacancies were at an all-time high, scandals and whistleblowers were still being suppressed and no one seemed to be accountable or in charge. There were specific warnings in 2011 that fragmentation of public health services would make us poorly prepared for a pandemic – and here we are. So there is a clear rationale for the right reform.

Hail Hancock

THE best part of the proposals is that "the NHS should be free to make decisions on how it organises itself without the involvement of the Competition and Markets Authority". Instead, the proposed reform reinstates power to the health secretary, which makes sense for a tax-funded service. But it makes it all the more important to install a wise, compassionate, scientifically literate leader, or we could end up with another Lansley, beavering away on an immensely complicated, cunning plan that doesn't work.

Hancock's new powers and capacity to meddle with the NHS would be considerable. He could replace NHS CEO Simon Stevens with Dido Harding. He could continue to buy goods and services (pandemic or otherwise) from his friends and contacts. He could sell our data. He could push more money into pet projects even if they had no evidence base or approval from the National Institute for Health and Care Excellence (NICE). He could get rid of NICE, the Care Quality Commission or even NHS England itself, possibly without primary legislation. And he could offer Serco, Sitel, Capita and a horde of management consultants a share of the tax pickings. Just as the Covid Act has allowed the government to make almost any emergency resource allocation decision without scrutiny or tender, Hancock will pick up this baton.

Stevens's big idea behind the reforms is to join up the NHS, public health services and social care into regional integrated care systems by statute, which hopefully will mean these vast chunks of care will stay public and can't be outsourced. Whether they will be transparent and accountable, help pandemic recovery, resolve urgent problems with staffing, social care and health inequalities, and deliver the myriad lefty promises Johnson made to get elected, we shall see. Stevens is due to stand down soon. The competence of his replacement is crucial. And a lot depends on Hancock. Has his pandemic performance earned him the right to more power?

---

2 February: UK has administered 10m doses of Covid vaccine. A study suggests OAZ vaccine gives protection for at least three months and cuts virus transmission by two-thirds. Captain Sir Tom Moore dies, aged 100, after testing positive for Covid-19. Nicola Sturgeon announces a phased return to school for Scotland's youngest schoolchildren from 22 Feb. **3 Feb**: Vets in Germany say they have trained sniffer dogs to detect coronavirus in human saliva with 94 percent accuracy. Switzerland withholds approval of OAZ vaccine pending more data; Belgium limits usage to under-55s. **4 Feb**: Netherlands limits OAZ vaccine to under-65s. **6 Feb**: AstraZeneca warns that its vaccine has reduced efficacy against South African variant. **7 Feb**: Government rules out vaccine passports. **8 Feb**: UK records 333 deaths – lowest for six weeks. **10 Feb**: WHO endorses use of OAZ vaccine on over-65s with a gap of 8-12 weeks, after some European countries restrict its use to under-65s. **12 Feb**: Figures show UK economy shrank by record 9.9% in 2020. **14 Feb**: 15m Britons have now received a first vaccine dose. 15 Feb: Hotel quarantine begins in England for arrivals from 33 high-risk countries.

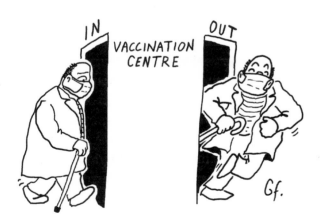

MD on Covid's legal fallout

Private Eye 1542   Press day: 1 March
6,685 daily cases   **255** daily deaths   **122,953** UK deaths to date

Data not dates

"DATA not dates" is the correct approach to managing a pandemic, provided the data is complete, correctly interpreted and consensually obtained. Overall, vaccines are leading to impressive reductions in infections and hospitalisations, but drug companies do not release all their ongoing trial data in real time, which makes it harder for regulators to spot potential problems. Meanwhile NHS records are a treasure trove of real-world data to help understand long Covid, and much else, but the data must be anonymised and used with consent, or the government risks another care.data fiasco (*Eye* 1360).

Much is still unpredictable. Setting staggered provisional dates for reopening the UK, depending on the data, will need continued support for people and industries facing financial ruin. But having spent a year over-promising and under-delivering, Boris Johnson could pull off the reverse if the data improves quicker than anticipated.

Working model

THE UK vaccine programme continues to deliver, with a single dose of either Pfizer-BioNTech or Oxford-AstraZeneca (OAZ) vaccine resulting in substantial reductions in infection, symptomatic illness and hospital admissions after three to four weeks. Two doses provide even better protection, particularly for the elderly; but for those aged 80 or over in Scotland, a single dose was associated with an 81 percent reduction in hospital admission risk in the fourth week. This suggests that staggering the doses to cover more people was a good call. Also, older people in Scotland mostly get the OAZ vaccine, which should give Germany, France and Belgium pause for thought...

Wilful stupidity

JOY at the success of the OAZ vaccine is tinged with despair that some EU governments have promoted vaccine scepticism by raising unfounded concerns about it. Germany started it. On 25 January, a German newspaper quoted a minister who claimed it was "only 8 percent effective in the elderly". President Emmanuel Macron of France then suggested it was second class. On 28 January, Germany said the over-65s should not have the jab because of "insufficient data to assess its efficacy".

Angela Merkel (66) has publicly declined it for herself, and Belgium has decreed it shouldn't be given to the over-55s. True, the OAZ trial data for the elderly was scant; but the European Medicines Agency, the WHO and the UK's Medicines and Healthcare products Regulatory Agency said it should be used in this age group, now backed up by impressive real-world data. Alas, the doubts are very hard to reverse and people of all ages in the EU are declining it and demanding the Pfizer jab (which, coincidentally, was developed in Germany and is manufactured in Germany and Belgium. The French Sanofi vaccine has yet to appear).

As of 19 February, just 150,000 out of 1.5m doses of the AstraZeneca jab had been used in Germany. At vaccination centres in Berlin that only give the OAZ vaccine, fewer than 200 people are turning up for the 3,800 daily appointments. Overall, 7 percent of German and French citizens have been vaccinated compared to 30 percent of Brits.

Individual EU countries have always had the power to set the bar of individual vaccine approval wherever they wished, but to see their citizens suffer and die as a result is beyond stupid, particularly when the UK data is looking so good. Meanwhile, Germany and France still have large waves of infection, and Belgium has even higher death rates per capita than the UK.

Vitamin D-Day

MANY doctors are taking vitamin D every day in the hope of reducing the risk or harm of Covid, but the jury is still out. Small, imperfect studies suggest impressive benefits, but better, larger studies find very few. Definitive randomised controlled trials are under way. MD has taken 10 micrograms of vitamin D every day for years, because it's hard to get enough naturally, especially in winter. I've also had a dose of vaccine. If I somehow still get severe Covid, I'd ask to be included in whatever trials are going on at the time (including extra vitamin D).

Missing inquiry

ONE thing missing from the third and hopefully final route map out of lockdown was the announcement of a public inquiry. Unless we fully understand what went right and what went wrong and why, we are likely to sleepwalk into the next pandemic. The UK has one of the worst mortality rates for Covid. But instead of just blaming politicians, we all – health professionals, managers, scientists, social media companies, tech and data companies, PPE and test providers, ventilation engineers, journalists, broadcasters and citizens – need to consider what we could have done better. The independent global inquiry into the performance of the World Health Organization, and the response of its member states, is due to report in May. A UK inquiry should follow soon afterwards, building on its findings.

Dial BMJ for Murder

THERE are two extreme views on the UK's pandemic management and 125,000 deaths. Boris Johnson believes that: "We truly did everything we could, and continue to do everything that we can, to minimise loss of life and to minimise suffering." The *British Medical Journal* – hardly a fringe publication – takes a different view: "Should Covid deaths be seen as 'social murder'? Or failing that, as crimes against humanity, involuntary manslaughter, misconduct in public office or criminal negligence? Politicians must be held to account by any constitutional means necessary."

According to the *BMJ* (13 Feb), "social murder" is a wilful refusal by government to address the social determinants and inequities of health, which have led to a disproportionate number of deaths among the poor and marginalised, including BAME communities. Certainly, successive governments have failed to enact the Equality Act, which includes a duty to address socio-economic disadvantage. This is at the heart of much pandemic death and suffering.

Sooner the better

GIVEN how the pandemic threat is continuing, we need a rapid interim report before next winter, when the risk will be highest. This happened after Hillsborough in 1989, allowing life-saving measures to be introduced in stadiums ahead of the next football season, but with the whole truth taking a lot longer to emerge. It would allow the government to acknowledge properly the scale of Covid and non-Covid deaths, loss and harm, and to learn urgent lessons to prepare us better. Any NHS reforms should also be guided by the inquiry's findings. Meanwhile, a huge wave of pandemic litigation and legislation is building up...

Wave one litigation

THE government is rushing through reforms and contracts under cover of the pandemic, without proper scrutiny, and then trying to keep them secret.

Following a Good Law Project challenge, health secretary Matt Hancock has already been found to have acted unlawfully by failing to publish multibillion-pound Covid-19 government contracts within the 30-day period required by law. Hancock has also been asked to refer Centene's takeover of GP services in London serving 500,000 patients for a Care Quality Commission investigation to determine if the private provider is up to the task of taking on such a large chunk of NHS work.

Open Democracy has just issued a lawsuit over the government's £23m NHS data deal with controversial "spy tech" company Palantir. Data sharing is crucial but the proposed NHS reforms mean much of the infrastructure is likely to be managed by big tech firms without public debate or consent.

A judicial review, meanwhile, is trying to get full disclosure of all documentation and decisions surrounding Cygnus, the government's pandemic preparedness plan. Was it ignored because of austerity cuts? We do not know.

Legal protection for staff

NHS staff want indemnity and protection from any litigation pursuant to patient harm, death or denial of treatment during the pandemic because they were doing their best in exceptionally dangerous circumstances, and don't deserve to be hung out to dry for systemic failures (see the case of Dr Hadiza Bawa-Garba, *Eye* 1466). Doctors are also arguing for better whistleblowing protection so they can fulfil their legal duty to raise concerns about dangerous care (the case of whistleblowing junior doctor Chris Day, *Eye* 1487, has yet to be resolved, but he has carried on serving patients on the pandemic frontline despite having his career ruined for raising concerns about unsafe practices and staffing in intensive care).

Compensation for harm

HOSPITALS, meanwhile, face litigation for the many cases where Covid was acquired within their walls. Care homes face litigation for letting the virus in – and may in turn countersue hospitals, the government and NHS England for forcing them to take untested, infected patients. NHS and care home workers are suing the government and employers for lack of testing and inadequate PPE in the face of a known deadly, biological hazard at work. Proving that infection happened in the workplace will be a protracted legal affair.

Non-Covid harms

FAMILIES of those who have suffered or died with non-Covid conditions because they couldn't get the care or support they needed during the pandemic are suing GPs, hospitals and care services. Students are suing to recover costs and lost education. Asymptomatic citizens are even suing the government for denying them the right to work because they tested positive for Covid when there is no accepted measure of how a positive test relates to infectiousness. And there will be claims too for alleged vaccine harm, and harms from novel, experimental treatments.

The legal system, like the NHS, was struggling to cope with demand before Covid, so what should the government do to avoid drowning in litigation? One option is a pandemic amnesty, offering compensation and support to those who have suffered, commensurate to their needs and without a protracted legal battle to prove accountability or negligence. The vast majority of public servants are decent, exhausted and doing their pandemic best. Litigation could be the final straw.

No jab, no job?

THE issues of mandatory vaccination and vaccine passports are so legally and ethically complex they require far more than a review by Michael Gove. MD is against mandatory vaccination of whole populations but had to have hepatitis B vaccinations to work as a doctor, which is appropriate for anyone who performs or assists at exposure-prone procedures that risk infecting patients. Covid vaccination take-up has been poorest for NHS and care workers, and previous calls for mandatory flu vaccination have been resisted. There will undoubtedly be legal challenges to whatever Gove's group decides. Better to air them at an inquiry.

---

17 February: A study shows the pandemic added $24tn to global debt in 2020. German authorities raise concern over public reluctance to receive OAZ vaccine. **19 Feb**: Government broke the law by failing to publish details of PPE spending within 30 days of contracts being awarded, a court finds. **20 Feb**: Government says all UK adults to be offered a first dose of vaccine by end of July. **22 Feb**: Government plans to lift England out of lockdown over a period of months, with schools reopening and outdoor socialising with one other person allowed from 8 March. Data shows a 70% fall in Covid-19 transmissions among UK healthcare workers who have received first dose of Pfizer vaccine. **23 Feb**: PM announces a review into idea of vaccine passports. **25 Feb**: UK Covid alert level lowered from 5 to 4. **27 Feb**: UK sees lowest number of cases in five months.

*"Good evening and welcome to the
Covid Blame Game"*

MD on Pressing priorities

Private Eye 1543   **Press day: 15 March**
5,601 daily cases   **108** daily deaths   **125,580 UK** deaths to date

Gathering evidence

MD has previously cautioned against large outdoor gatherings in a pandemic, but there have now been so many – on beaches, and in celebration and protest – that evidence of risk has now emerged. As chief scientific adviser Sir Patrick Vallance told MPs last week: "Nothing is completely risk free. It is the case that it is difficult to see how things like large beach gatherings and so on can cause a spike. The same was the case in a protest march in New York. They did not really see any spikes after that."

The problem is that large-scale outdoor meetings, such as last year's Cheltenham Festival, were combined with lots of indoor pub celebrations, restaurant visits and people piling on to crowded trains and buses. But it's fair to say a peaceful, dignified, largely masked outdoor vigil in memory of Sarah Everard, highlighting violence against women, was always going to be low risk, and shutting it down using violence against women was unwise, if legal.

A nation divided

BRITAIN, as ever, is divided. The rich and mobile want to move on quickly from the pandemic, have already booked two summer holidays (one abroad and one in the UK, just in case) and are chuffed that they invested in vaccine companies. Many are breaking the rules already. They aren't remotely interested in a public inquiry, just grateful for the vaccines in more ways than one.

Then there are those struggling to move on from the pandemic, either because of grief or long-term medical or economic harm, and they want answers and acknowledgement in an inquiry so we don't make the same mistakes again. The government, meanwhile, doesn't want anyone to look in great detail at why the UK has suffered 125,000 Covid deaths and counting. Time to move on and upset the nurses…

Nurse! The screams…

THE government has argued since 2010 that it is better to employ more nurses on lower pay than to give existing nurses a decent pay rise. So it's no surprise Boris Johnson is doing so again, even though some of our most experienced nurses have less to spend since the Conservatives came to power. In 2010/11, the top of the band 5 pay scale for nurses was £27,534, and in 2019/20 it had risen to £30,112. After adjusting for inflation, this represents a 9 percent real-terms fall.

Johnson chose to exploit photos of shattered nurses with mask-pocked faces for the "Can you look them in the eyes and tell them you're doing all you can to stop the spread of Covid-19?" poster campaign. So he can't complain if the nursing unions counter with: "Can you look them in the eyes and tell them they're not worth more than a 1% pay rise?" With around 35,000 NHS nursing vacancies, Johnson is banking on nursing applications going up regardless, both out of inspiration and desperation as alternative jobs disappear.

However, the key problem in the NHS is retaining staff. Many go into the job with the best intentions but leave when they are so over-stretched they cannot provide the safe, high quality, compassionate care they envisaged when training. They are at constant risk of suspension and litigation for mistakes made while working in such an unsafe system. And then there is the Covid risk. A larger pay rise would not change this; but given the exhaustion, post-traumatic stress and long-Covid symptoms staff are suffering, it would at least have acknowledged how valued and vital their work is.

So what should nurses do? One thing health secretary Matt Hancock and prime minister Johnson can't live without is their jocular and matey photo-op elbow bumps with NHS staff that makes it look like they're in charge of the vaccine programme and everybody in the NHS loves them for it. Turn your back on them. Don't give them the elbow. Or rather, do.

Teachers first

ALL frontline staff should have priority vaccination. This is not because they are at higher risk of death but because they are moving and perhaps spreading around communities to provide essential services that would cease if they went off sick with Covid. This applies particularly to teachers. The welfare of children should be paramount. If we foul our nest, we foul our future. Any teacher who catches Covid can't teach, so their students will fall even further behind. We should vaccinate teachers to protect children's education. This would have the added benefit of rewarding and reassuring those re-entering crowded classrooms with poor ventilation and new variants afoot.

Priority ventilation

SCHOOLS must stay safe to stay open. For an airborne virus, this means keeping the air flowing.

In the US, the Centers for Disease Control and Prevention (CDC) has issued detailed guidance for schools and childcare, urging the opening of windows, the use of portable air cleaners and child-safe fans, and improved building-wide filtration. Heating, ventilation and air conditioning (HVAC) settings must maximise ventilation to bring as much outdoor air into classrooms as the system will safely allow. The aim is to improve air filtration as much as possible without significantly reducing airflow. The use of portable air cleaners with high-efficiency particulate air (HEPA) filters is encouraged where possible. Activities, classes and lunches should be outdoors when circumstances allow.

In the UK, by contrast, filtered, flowing air is not seen as a priority. The typical state-school classroom contains 31 people and has poor ventilation; and teaching periods last up to two hours before children and teachers leave for a break. No wonder the chief medical officer for England Chris Whitty is already predicting another surge.

Test priorities

THE UK government abandoned community testing at the start of the pandemic but rebounded by spending £37bn with the aim of providing outsourced "moonshot" testing for the entire population. The Commons public accounts committee verdict is damning: "Despite the unimaginable resources thrown at this project, NHS Test and Trace cannot point to a measurable difference to the progress of the pandemic, and the promise on which this huge expense was justified — avoiding another lockdown — has been broken, twice." NHS Test and Trace must also "wean itself off its persistent reliance on consultants and temporary staff".

So why is Test and Trace not delivering when the vaccination programme is? Vaccinations have the massive advantage of using an existing NHS database to trace patients, and tried and tested NHS roll-out programmes used every year for flu. Test and Trace had to build its own database and employed temporary, outsourced staff who had never done this type of work before. Hancock's hubris and faith in technology led him to believe he could build a better app than Apple or Google, and control a highly complex and uncertain operation from the centre.

The other huge advantage of vaccines is that people generally want one, whereas they don't want to be told they have a positive test, particularly if they have no symptoms, and be ordered to isolate at home for no (or less) money and cough up all their contacts. Many people don't answer the phone, turn their tracing app off or just don't do as they're ordered. The government keeps crowing about how many tests it does – more than any other country – but these make no difference to infection rates if you can't persuade people to do the right thing. This is why Test and Trace should have remained within the NHS and local authorities, where local experts would have stood a better chance of controlling local outbreaks.

Finally, test results can be hard to interpret. The accuracy of testing changes with disease prevalence. If you do mass testing when infection levels are low, as now, you get far more false results. Many – perhaps most – of the positive lateral flow tests results in school are currently false, and not always being checked with a more accurate PCR test. Even

if that is negative, in some schools the entire class bubble is still ordered to isolate at home for 10 days. This makes no sense to MD.

Priority PPE

IN the NHS 77 percent of staff are women and yet their personal protective equipment was designed for men and doesn't fit or protect women as well, the *BMJ* reports. Female staff say that goggles slip, gowns are too long, face shields push against breasts, and respirators don't fit their faces. Much of the most protective equipment is designed with Caucasian men in mind so BAME women often fail "fit tests" on two accounts, and have to choose between sharing powered respirators (often in short supply and inadequately cleaned), or wearing items that simply don't fit and let the virus through. Very few feel brave enough to refuse to work when staff levels are so low and patient demand so high. An inquiry is needed to see if this has contributed to staff illness and death from Covid.

The solution – to design bespoke respirators and PPE – is more expensive; but 3D printing is already being used to develop personalised respirators from facial scans. Globally, hospitals with the best PPE have had fewer staff deaths and less intra-hospital spread. The government must decide whether personalised PPE is a priority.

Public fatness

PUBLIC health has never been a priority in the UK. We have shocking levels of obesity and this has contributed to shocking levels of death when the virus was allowed to spread. Ninety percent of global deaths have occurred in countries with high rates of obesity. No country with high death rates has less than 50 percent of its population overweight. Vietnam has the lowest Covid death rate in the world and the second lowest level of overweight people; the UK has the third highest death rate in the world and the fourth highest obesity rate. It doesn't prove cause and effect, but it's highly suspicious.

In the UK, 80 percent of adults carry excess body fat and so are at high risk of premature death not just from Covid but diabetes, heart disease, cancer, liver disease, kidney disease and suicide. You name it, obesity increases your risk of it. Tackling it should be a priority.

Global priorities

THE pandemic reminds us how connected we all are, and that health emergencies in one country can impact every country. One hundred and thirty-four countries signed up for the WHO's "Health for All by the year 2000" but didn't deliver. In desperation, the WHO has now moved to declaring "Health Threats for All" and with extraordinary prescience made 2109 "the year of preparedness for global health emergencies". Was the world listening?

High threat pathogens (including SARS) were just one item on the top 10 watch list. And there are seven statements that were always predictable about this pandemic and the next:

- Likely to be a virus – very small, very transmissible, not always easy to detect and the little buggers mutate all the time.
- Likely to come from animals – they harbour millions of viruses we've never seen before, and humans breed, transport, slaughter and eat all manner of animals in very insanitary circumstances. We also destroy their natural habitats (forests) and displace them closer to us.
- Likely to spread human to human, and in the air. Having jumped from animals, mutations that learn to spread quickly between humans are likely to be selected to thrive.
- Likely to start in a country where public health surveillance is rudimentary, where poverty, hunger and economics mean natural resources are exploited to the full, leading to gross changes in local ecology. Other persistent risks are over-crowding, insanitary cultural practices and a culture of political cover-up. Not just China.
- Likely to travel by plane and to be all over our hyper-connected world before the country of origin owns up.
- Likely to kill the poorest, most marginalised and least healthy in the greatest numbers.
- Likely to be better managed in countries with less inequality, better population health and better public health services.

Rich countries need to increase and target their foreign aid. And unless the WHO uses its reinstated US funding to reboot health for all, with global support to address these issues, another pandemic is highly likely. The UK, alas, is one of the most unequal rich countries where thousands of people die prematurely from all sorts of avoidable diseases every year. So no surprise we have had so many avoidable deaths from Covid.

Bullet point

NOW that we're starting Groundhog Year again, we are at least doing so with the benefit of vaccines and much better (though not perfect) testing. However, unless vaccines are made available to the world, we could soon be playing Russian roulette again... but this time with Covid-variant bullets.

---

3 March: Chancellor Rishi Sunak predicts "swifter and more sustained" economic recovery and extends furlough to September. **4 Mar:** Survey shows 49 percent of over-80s who have had two vaccine doses have since broken lockdown rules. Germany and Sweden recommend OAZ vaccine for over-65s. Italy and Germany announce plans to give just one vaccine dose to people who have had Covid-19 in the past six months. **7 Mar:** England invites people aged 55-59 for vaccinations. **8 Mar:** Schools reopen across England. NHS Nightingale hospitals in England to close in April. **9 Mar:** 17 European countries pause use of a batch of OAZ vaccine that resulted in a death in Austria. **11 Mar:** MHRA stresses there is no evidence to link OAZ vaccine to increased risk of blood clots. **14 Mar:** The Netherlands suspends use of OAZ vaccine. **15 Mar:** Italy, France, Portugal, Slovenia and Cyprus suspend use of OAZ vaccine pending assessment by EU regulator. WHO says there is no evidence to link OAZ vaccine to blood clots.

MD on Life after death

Private Eye **1544**   **Press day: 29 March**

4,570 daily cases   46 daily deaths   **126,615** UK deaths to date

Remembrance day

23 MARCH, the anniversary of the first lockdown, was as good a day as any to remember those lost to and harmed by the pandemic.

Research by the Health Foundation estimates the true figure for UK Covid deaths so far is 146,000 and that each life was cut short by up to ten years (6.5 years for the over-75s). People in the most deprived parts of England were twice as likely to die from Covid-19, and they also died at younger ages. Many had pre-existing health conditions.

Covid has exacerbated existing inequalities. The rich have been able to stay safe at home thanks to the poor delivering to our doors. Instead of just focusing on Covid, we need to focus on preventing *all* premature death and disease, whatever the cause. Covid has also taught us that no amount of healthcare can reverse an unhealthy environment or self-destructive behaviour.

Early deaths happen not just from environmental exposure to SARS-CoV-2, but cigarettes, drugs, air pollution, alcohol, junk food, sedentary lifestyles, accidents, abuse and despair. Globally, nearly 3m people have died from Covid, but 57m have died from causes that didn't get a daily death update. Millions of these lives could have been saved with decent public health and universal healthcare. Far from being a drain on the economy, investing in and protecting health are fundamental to it. Another key lesson of Covid.

Bug's Law

THE International Health Regulations 2005 (IHR 2005) were agreed by 194 member states of the World Health Organization after the SARS outbreak of 2002/3, placing a legal obligation on them to urgently report to the WHO any event "which may constitute a public health emergency of international concern". Outbreaks of four named critical diseases have to be reported in all circumstances. Smallpox, poliomyelitis due to wild type poliovirus, human influenza caused by a new subtype, and severe acute respiratory syndrome (SARS). Many legal experts believe the Chinese government violated this law by delaying reporting the initial SARS-CoV-2 outbreak in December 2019, perhaps by a month. China argues that it took time to confirm the virus type, and it provided the entire genomic sequence on 12 January 2020, allowing vaccine development to start immediately and a PCR virus test to be developed on 16 January which should have allowed all countries to stop the outbreak, as China did. The UK, US and many others were simply not prepared.

Sanctioning China and keeping it on board to stop the next outbreak is problematic. And IHR 2005 also applies to any SARS-CoV-2 variants of concern.

Border control

NOW that vaccines and lockdowns have got infection rates right down, the government must decide if it wants to keep UK borders as virus-tight as it can without inviting economic ruin. This might mean compensating the travel industry but cautiously opening up domestic sports stadia, entertainment venues, shops, pubs, restaurants and holiday venues.

Worryingly, a large South African trial has found that two doses of the Oxford-AstraZeneca vaccine "did not show protection against mild-to-moderate Covid-19 due to the B.1.351 [South African] variant". There were no cases of serious disease or death among trial participants, who were largely young. South Africa needs to keep using the vaccine in the elderly to see how much it reduces death. Clearly vaccine tweaks and boosters will be needed, and we may not now be holidaying abroad this summer. Evidence suggests all the variants travel by plane. But how much border control will UK citizens tolerate?

Scotland has touted a zero-Covid policy, and almost got there last summer. It has done better than England on excess deaths but hasn't been able to maintain zero. The virus has spread so widely as to become firmly embedded, with many global feeding and breeding stations to develop and select new variants. Vaccination will reduce deaths, but the virus is likely to remain one step ahead.

Vaccinating to the max

THE UK is "vaccinating to the max" to minimise the harm of the virus, but that won't reverse health inequalities. Some of those at highest risk are still declining a vaccine by arguing: "The state has screwed me over many times before, so why should I trust it now?" Public health works best in an environment of trust and consent. Vaccines should remain voluntary except in jobs or situations where the risk of transmission is very high.

UK uptake overall has been impressive. Uncontrolled spread of the Kent variant earned us the moniker of "Plague Island" in December and January. Now it is the rest of Europe that has become "plague continent", thanks to their poorly executed vaccine plan and super-spread of the, er, Kent variant.

We are all in this together. We have now given more than half our adult population half the scheduled dose, with a few million having both doses, and none yet to children. So there is still plenty of potential for UK spread and variation. But once we have vaccinated our most vulnerable citizens twice, it's entirely right that the rest of Europe, and the world, should be allowed to catch up. If not, we may soon re-import a Kent-meets-Bruges variant.

The EU claims the UK "has given it nothing", but we helped install bioreactors at the Halix vaccine factory in Leyden, Holland; we supply a crucial component of the Pfizer vaccine; and we invested heavily in developing the Oxford-AstraZeneca (OAZ) vaccine using UK taxes, expertise and trial volunteers, made available to the world at cost price and easy to store in a fridge. Alas, even if the EU had enough OAZ vaccine for all its citizens, many would now refuse to have it.

Vaccine safety

IN the midst of a third wave, thousands of EU citizens will die and be harmed by refusing a life-saving vaccine which may, but probably doesn't, harm a tiny fraction of them. The balance of benefit and risk is greatly in favour of urgent vaccination, yet millions of doses are unused. Why?

Having already (wrongly) judged the OAZ vaccine to be ineffective in the elderly, some EU countries temporarily suspended its use because of an alleged increase in clotting risk. The European Medicines Agency (EMA) found no increase in clots overall. Indeed, there are more clots in those unvaccinated. The EMA did find the vaccine may be associated with a very rare type of blood clot, but the risk of clots overall, long-term harm and death is far higher if you get Covid. In the UK, 20m OAZ doses have been safely given and it has already led to a 60-70 percent risk reduction in symptomatic Covid and more than 80 percent decrease in severe cases.

Alas, once you damage a vaccine's reputation, it rarely recovers. Angela Merkel knows this. She will also know that lifting the suspension and belatedly agreeing to have the OAZ vaccine herself, having decried it on two counts previously, won't change many minds. "The British vaccine" has been declared second-rate in Europe. AstraZeneca's shares have tumbled.

Risk communication

IT's clearly important to monitor any new vaccines that use new technologies and will be given to billions of people. The UK Medicines and Healthcare products Regulatory Agency and the EMA should give regular public briefings on vaccine benefits and risks as they unfold: how many vaccines have been given; our best estimate of their contribution in reducing death, disease and spread; recorded adverse events; and the adverse events we would expect in a population that hadn't received the vaccine.

They should do this for every one of the Covid vaccines, not just pick on the British one, whenever important new data emerges. Far better for people who understand the science to communicate the science, rather than protective EU leaders bitter about Brexit.

Greed not so good?

THE UK wasn't prepared for a pandemic and so splashed £12.5bn on PPE in 2020 that would have cost £2.5bn at 2019 prices, and was largely imported from… China. The government will not disclose the contracts or profits made by deal brokers, despite a legal obligation to do so.

For all this hugely expensive "personal protection", 900 health and care staff have died after contracting Covid (though not all at work), more than 450 people a day caught Covid while in hospital in January 2021, and more than 40,000 in total. Clearly, we need to rethink healthcare-acquired Covid. Better ventilation and barriers may be needed.

Meanwhile, Boris Johnson's paltry 1 percent pay rise for NHS nurses (4 percent in Scotland) will drive more into agency working, where they can earn three times as much per hour, doing the same job. The NHS also has to pay a large slice to the agency, with a total cost of up to six times that of a salaried nurse.

Long Covid

MD works in an NHS service for young people with ME/chronic fatigue syndrome and knows how they can struggle to be believed. Long Covid could repeat this prejudice or be a golden opportunity to research the long-term damage a viral infection can inflict on the body, and to develop new treatments. It will be a very heterogeneous condition, with some sufferers having end organ damage after intensive care, and others with extreme fatigue but normal routine investigations.

No one can say how long any individual's long Covid will last, but we need to learn from those who are fortunate enough to recover fully. Paul Garner, a professor at the Liverpool School of Tropical Medicine, caught Covid and blogged about it for the *British Medical Journal*: "I felt so unwell I thought I was dying. The roller-coaster that followed lasted for months…"

Garner, however, has since made a full recovery by increasing his activities when he felt ready, and not suffering severe payback. Yet others in his situation are finding any such increase leaves them with profound post-exertional malaise. This is also true of the ME/CFS patients I see. Some make a full recovery, some reach a plateau and stay there, and others appear to recover and then get relapses.

ME/CFS diagnosis, research and treatment are hampered because we don't yet have a diagnostic blood test. The same is true for long Covid. It needs a definition agreed by patients and doctors, and NICE needs to develop guidelines for treatment.

Bugs and us

INFECTIOUS diseases have altered the course of history far more than war, but they are not all bad. Their evolutionary challenge has helped us evolve, and many technological advances will follow the Covid challenge. Our bodies contain trillions of microbes living harmoniously in huge communities in our gut and respiratory tract, and on our skin. Our relationship with them is both essential to our existence and highly complex. Environment, as ever, is key. Microbes thrive and help us thrive in one part of our body, but kill us if they end up in another. Gut bugs in the gut, good. Gut bugs in the blood or brain, dead.

Over the centuries, our struggle with microbes has delivered some haymaker blows but as yet no knockout, apart from smallpox. We should be in awe of the evolutionary ingenuity that has allowed microbes to adapt, survive and flourish in the face of all we've thrown at them. SARS-CoV-2 doesn't have enough genetic material to be "evil" or "malign". It exists only to spread, and we have given it the opportunity.

Yes, it can kill us, but largely because our fickleness, selfishness and short memories have allowed it to. We didn't learn the lessons of SARS-CoV-1 in 2003. Nearly all our health is determined by our environment, and 7.8bn hungry humans determine that environment more than any other species. We habitually destroy habitats that bring bugs and their animal hosts closer to us. In a sense, we get the bugs we deserve. And they usually win.

---

16 March: European Medicines Agency investigates 30 cases of unusual blood disorders among 5m recipients of OAZ vaccine. **17 Mar:** European Commission threatens to withhold vaccines from UK. **18 Mar:** EMA declares OAZ vaccine safe. Germany, Italy, France and others resume use. **22 Mar:** On the anniversary of the first lockdown, UK lights candles in remembrance of lives lost. **25 Mar:** UK emergency Covid regulations extended for six months. **27 Mar:** NHS England passes 25m first vaccine doses administered. **29 Mar:** Stay-at-home order in England ends – two households or six people may meet outside. France records highest number of patients in intensive care since November.

"Brace yourselves. We're coming in"

MD on Risks and rewards

Private Eye 1545   Press day 12 April

2,667 daily cases   **30** daily deaths   **127,100** UK deaths to date

Good news

ON 6 April, there were no Covid-19 hospital deaths reported in London, East of England or the South-west, and just two deaths in people aged 80-plus in all of England. New infections are very low or zero in large parts of the UK. More than 60 percent of the adult population has received one vaccine dose and more than 10 percent both doses. UK vaccines are estimated to have prevented 6,300 deaths, and many more hospital admissions, with far fewer side effects than lockdown.

Vaccine benefits v risks

IN the last year in the UK, 4.4m people have been infected with SARS-CoV-2 and there have been at least 127,000 deaths as a result. Imagine these 4.4m people had been fully immunised with the Oxford-AstraZeneca (OAZ) vaccine at the outset. At least 100,000 Covid deaths could have been prevented, and there would have been around 22 cases of a rare combination of blood clot and low platelets, with five deaths.

Compared to risk of a clot after vaccination, you are six times more likely to be struck by lightning in your lifetime, 11 times more likely to die in a car accident each year and 100 times more likely to get a blood clot if you use an oral contraceptive. If you are hospitalised with Covid, your risk of a clot is one in four.

Three of the 19 who died from thrombosis following 20.2m doses of the OAZ vaccination were under 30, and those aged 29 and under will now be offered a different vaccine (though other vaccines may have similar tiny risks). In future, vaccine supply may be sufficient for people to choose which vaccine they have, but not yet. Will this put people off having a vaccine? With infection rates currently very low (thanks to vaccines), some may decide to wait for more safety data to emerge or hope herd immunity will protect them without a vaccine. This strategy is much riskier than having the vaccine, particularly in the long term.

Many of those who volunteered for vaccine trials when the risks were unknown were under 30. Some volunteered to be deliberately infected with SARS-CoV-2 to help improve our understanding. Many are likely to have a vaccine not just for personal protection, but to protect friends and family, open up society, boost the economy, allow travel and encourage further medical advances from the new vaccine technology. Some people get unpleasant temporary side effects from the vaccines. But the overall chance of dying, as with just about every modern vaccine, is around one in a million. Paracetamol is much more of a risk.

European differences

WHY did, say, Germany spot and act more quickly on the rare risks associated with the OAZ vaccine?

The mistaken belief that the vaccine was less effective in the elderly meant it was diverted to younger age cohorts where the risk of clotting is more evident (though still very low). Their better-resourced health system may also be more meticulous in picking up and reporting adverse reactions.

The UK has a Yellow Card reporting scheme anyone can access, but it's a bit hit-and-miss. Rare, life-threatening events tend to be picked up, but less serious effects depend on people reporting them. The Germans may be more thorough and risk averse. Hence they, and other EU countries, are recommending a wider age range for OAZ restriction. But if it means people are denied an available life-saving vaccine during a third wave outbreak, the approach may do more harm than good.

Out of Africa

AFRICAN nations, with younger populations, may also move away from the OAZ vaccine; but it is cheap, easy to store and currently available. If the opt-out delays vaccination in areas with large outbreaks, this too is likely to result in far more deaths. The UK is much safer now than in winter, which saw 1,300 Covid deaths a day. Brazil has just hit 4,000 deaths in 24 hours. The good news is that China's CoronaVac vaccine has 73.8 percent efficacy against the Brazilian variant which accounts for 80 percent of Brazil's cases.

Chinese takeaway

AS predicted, the World Health Organization fact-finding team returned from China without all the facts. Its aim was to find the origin of the SARS-CoV-2 virus based on information the Chinese government shared with it. The very long report places the start of the outbreak "in the months before mid-December" 2019, when the virus could have been spreading undetected. It thinks it likely it was introduced to humans via an unknown animal that acted as an intermediary between bats, but it wasn't able to find that animal or a specific lineage of bats.

The SARS-CoV-2 virus can infect a very large number of animals, which is bad luck for humans because it gives it multiple opportunities to reinvent itself in future. It also means the "follow the animals" studies to find the original source will be lengthy and complex, and will need to extend beyond China.

Bats v labs

BATS are beautiful, they carry lots of viruses and they can fly long distances. They are also mammals, and the SARS-CoV-2 virus didn't have to adapt much to spread to human mammals, which is again bad luck for us. The virus picked up its infamous spike protein en route, but whether that was in a pangolin or a laboratory is currently impossible to say.

The WHO says the lab-leak hypothesis is "extremely unlikely", but it has happened before. The last naturally occurring case of smallpox was in 1977, but the last recorded death was 1978. Janet Parker, a medical photographer, contracted it while working at the smallpox laboratory at Birmingham Medical School, which the WHO had commissioned to research the disease.

What makes a lab leak less likely is that SARS-CoV-2 was unknown before the pandemic, and there is no trail in public databases or research articles of any lab virus like it. If it was being researched or modified, it had not been logged and declared, which could be administrative laxity, or the virus got to the researcher before they had a chance to log it, or it was a secret project.

The WHO wants more investigation and says "all hypotheses remain on the table", including the very unlikely ones. We may never find a smoking gun/bat/lab, but the closer we get to the origin, the better shot we have at prevention in future. Closing off outbreaks at source is the goal.

Dirtiest of dirty bombs

EVOLUTION is far better at producing bio-weapons than laboratories are, and it would be hard to design one as destructive, divisive and disruptive as the SARS-CoV-2 virus. It spread silently and quickly among the young and healthy to start with, before detonating in the elderly and those unlucky enough to be susceptible.

Covid has killed 3m people and caused an extremely unpleasant chronic disease in millions more. But its management has harmed the lives and livelihoods of billions and led to a massive spike in waiting times for non-Covid illnesses.

Yet – more than a year later – there remain huge divisions among politicians, public health experts, the press and the public about how to manage it and many people are still living in fear. Vaccines will help us return to a semblance of normality. But do we need mass testing on top?

Moonshot a-go-go

BORIS Johnson's enthusiasm for mass testing is understandable. When the pandemic first hit Europe and the WHO (and MD) was screaming "test, test, test", the UK wasn't up to the task and abandoned community testing (*Eye* 1518). Stung by this, Johnson committed up to £37bn – of which £20bn might have been spent so far – on an outsourced test and trace programme that did more testing than other countries but struggled with contact tracing and supporting isolation. We weren't able to stop further lockdowns or a second wave killing nearly twice as many as the first.

A further complication is that around 30 percent of viral spread is asymptomatic. So Johnson's solution of offering bi-weekly self-tests to all asymptomatic adults in the UK, with results back in 30 minutes, sounds compelling. It could get some asymptomatic shedders off the street and provide mass reassurance to others, though some of it false. Like vaccine passports, a negative test doesn't guarantee you aren't infectious, it just reduces the likelihood.

Also, the public like the idea of having rapid access to rapid tests that give rapid results, and that – along with vaccines – should play well in local elections. It's also a great opportunity for someone to make a profit from up to 80m tests a week...

Self-testing on trial

THE ritualistic bi-weekly self-testing of asymptomatic adults has its potential downsides:

- Up to 40m people with no symptoms become medicalised for uncertain benefit.
- Could the money be better spent?
- Johnson has put up to £100bn into the Moonshot pot, when there are millions of patients waiting for treatments that have been proven to work. Could the money be better spent?
- While infection rates are so low, mass asymptomatic testing is unlikely to pick up many infections.
- We don't know how many people will do the tests properly when unsupervised at home, and log in the results online (which is a fiddle).
- Many people don't follow isolation rules even if they have symptoms, so expecting people to isolate unsupervised when they don't have symptoms is a stretch.
- Tracing contacts and persuading them to isolate is already a struggle. There is no point massively ramping up testing if we can't cope with the extra tracing work it triggers.
- Lateral flow tests (LFTs) aren't nearly as good as polymerase chain reaction (PCR) tests. A Cochrane review found LFTs pick up only 58 percent of asymptomatic cases and 72 percent of symptomatic ones. This may encourage risky behaviour in people who tested negative but are infectious.
- Millions of tests will be sent by post or click and collect, for an unspecified period. That's a big carbon footprint (there's a lot of plastic in the kits).
- Will the novelty wear off? Once people have been vaccinated, and infection rates are low, will they still self-test when they feel fine and don't need a test to enter a venue because they have proof of vaccination?

Lateral thinking

THE most accurate way to use LFTs is to help speed up existing test, trace and isolate services for those with symptoms. It will pick up many positives immediately – with a back-up PCR test – allowing immediate contact tracing and support for isolation. We might manage to get more infectious people out of circulation that way. If we continue to use them to screen staff in higher risk settings (schools, hospitals and universities), this needs to be part of a study.

An experiment in control

FOR all nations management of the pandemic has been a huge bio-psycho-social experiment in control. In the teeth of an outbreak, pragmatism rules. But when infection rates are low, we should properly design and evaluate interventions to learn if benefits outweigh risks. Instead, the government is advertising for "an interim head of asymptomatic testing communication who will primarily be responsible for delivering a communications strategy to support the expansion of asymptomatic testing, that normalises testing as part of everyday life". Instead of doing a controlled experiment, Johnson is continuing the experiment in control, with huge spend, little consent and no way of knowing the consequences.

---

30 March: Germany's vaccine regulator advises against giving under-60s OAZ vaccine. **1 April:** ONS survey suggests a fifth of people have "long Covid" symptoms five weeks after initial infection. **3 Apr:** Government says a Covid passport system will be trialled at various events from 16 April. **5 Apr:** PM confirms pubs, restaurants, hairdressers, gyms and non-essential shops in England can reopen from 12 April. **7 Apr:** Belgium announces plan to restrict use of OAZ vaccine to over-55s. Angela Merkel backs calls for short national lockdown as German cases rise. UK advises against OAZ vaccine for under-30s. A Carmarthen woman becomes first person in UK to receive Moderna vaccine. **9 Apr:** Pakistan and Bangladesh among countries added to UK's travel "red list". **12 Apr:** Non-essential shops, gyms and pubs reopen in England and Wales; Scotland and Northern Ireland ease some restrictions.

VACCINATION
PASSPORT
CHECK

"Bloody jabsworth!"

MD on Communicating Covid

Private Eye **1546**   **Press day: 26 April**

2,259 daily cases   **22** daily deaths   **127,434** UK deaths to date

Caught in a trap

SHOULD Boris Johnson be "more upbeat" in his presentation of pandemic data, as the *Telegraph* and others are now demanding? Certainly the UK data is looking good.

More than 50 percent of the UK population has had at least one dose of a vaccine and they are working, with SARS-CoV-2 infection rates, hospitalisation and deaths at their lowest for seven months. We bought and worked hard for our success, paying four times as much as some countries to get early access to the Pfizer vaccine, and investing heavily in developing and delivering the Oxford-AstraZeneca (OAZ) vaccine.

Staring down the barrel of 1,300 Covid deaths a day, we gambled on early vaccination before more safety data was available, and spacing out vaccines against manufacturers' recommendations to reach more people more quickly. These gambles have worked. Daily UK Covid admissions are down to double figures.

Alas, global infection rates have doubled in the past two months and are their highest ever. India, South America and mainland Europe are hardest hit. India has 5,000 Covid deaths a day and only 8.6 percent of the population has had a vaccine dose. There is a strong argument for suspending existing vaccine patents to allow poorer countries to manufacture their own (though the process is highly complex). There is an even stronger argument for using the OAZ vaccine globally, and for the UK and others to donate any excess.

Dominic Cummings appears keen to expose Johnson's pre-vaccination failures (late lockdowns; lack of border control), but Johnson, Donald Trump and Narendra Modi are not the only world leaders outsmarted and humbled by something 1/10,000th the diameter of this full stop. Johnson vowed to follow the data, and he could lift restrictions when all the most vulnerable have been offered second vaccines. But he will always need a safety net. A future vaccine-resistant variant could emerge by chance and require a temporary lockdown to reduce deaths while vaccines are adjusted. By declaring that his roadmap out of lockdown will be "irreversible", he has removed his safety net. It makes him a hostage to fortune again. No wonder he looks worried.

Of mice and men

THE role of chance in pandemics was well illustrated in controlled epidemic studies of mice by William Topley and Major Greenwood between 1920 and 1940. The pair admitted that "hundreds of thousands of mice were sacrificed" in their meticulous process of controlling myriad variables – type of infection, type of mouse, degree of overcrowding, "mousehold" size, the level of pre-existing immunity, nutrition, genetic variations, etc. The overriding conclusion is that even when you control as much as you possibly can, chance events contribute greatly to the patterns and speed of spread in epidemics. This is not surprising, given that viruses mutate at random. Alas, "some shit happens by chance" is the excuse history never forgives and the media never accepts.

Fear kills too

THE biggest communication challenge of this pandemic has been to get people to take all sensible measures to reduce the risk of infection and spread without scaring them senseless. We know fear is very bad for physical and mental health and can trigger heart attacks in those susceptible. Fear may be one reason 20,000 pupils appear to have fallen off the school register. GPs and hospitals are now seeing a steady stream of tragic "Covid delay" patients who were too frightened to seek help for "red flag" cancer symptoms and now have incurable disease.

As one woman explained: "I found this rock-hard lump in my breast in March [2020]. I knew what it was but I thought it could wait. A relative of mine had gone to hospital and caught Covid in hospital and died. I knew if I went to see my GP he would just send me to hospital, and I didn't want to die from Covid. Every day, I worried if I was doing the right thing or not. Some days, I would get as far as putting my coat on to go down to the GP, but then changing my mind…" She lived a life of fearful rumination until November before seeking help, and now has metastatic spread.

Alas, fear is an inevitable consequence of incompetence. We

weren't prepared for this pandemic but confidently believed we were. (The UK was ranked second in a global index of pandemic preparedness on 24 October 2019. The US was top – see *Eye* 1520.) When we realised the outbreak was out of control and we needed to lock down, Johnson's manner turned overnight from upbeat to fearful, and fear has been used as a tactic to enforce compliance with the restrictions ever since, with scary advertising campaigns, fines and threats of imprisonment, and relentless coverage of Covid deaths and daily death updates. In such a climate of fear, an advert reminding you to get a breast lump checked did not break through.

NHS protection

IN an ideal world, the health service should protect the people, not rely on the people to protect it. This would require a big increase in capacity and staffing, rather than routinely running it at close to 100 percent capacity. Instead of being overwhelmed by a single disease, we could have split sites into Covid and non-Covid centres. Everyone would know where to go with their breast lump, and the risk of contracting Covid there would be very small.

We paid a fortune to build Nightingale hospitals and requisition private hospitals for, say, cancer care, but they also rely on NHS staff to run them and so were barely used. Covid and non-Covid patients ended up sharing the same hospitals and more than 40,000 people who didn't have Covid on admission caught it there. Much of the fear around Covid was justified by our inability to control it: 150,000 lives may have been shortened by Covid, and the cancer figures may be equally shocking. Johnson is right not to be too upbeat.

No rush

WOULD a jolly Boris Johnson increase footfall on the high street? Possibly not. Prolonged lockdown has been a huge psychological experiment with many unknown consequences. Some people may be fearful and anxious about returning to shops, many will be worried about their finances with the end of furlough, and some have got into the habit of not buying – or needing – so much stuff.

People will still turn out for what matters to them (a murdered woman; a dead royal; a destructive European Super League), but now the shopping shackles are off, footfall in non-food stores is still well below 2019 levels. Whether that is due to lack of confidence, cash or consumer desire remains to be seen. Eating out is also down on April 2019, but that could be fear of hypothermia in a chilly spring as much as fear of crowds. The relentless "stay at home" message is taking a while to reverse.

Mental health

MULTIPLE surveys and calls to charities suggest the pandemic has made mental health worse, but as yet there was no increase in rates of suicide in the UK up to October 2020 (except perhaps in young people). This has been observed in other countries too (although Japan has seen a rise). There may yet be variations between demographic groups or geographical areas, but the crisis may have fostered a sense of social cohesion to fight an external threat, as exemplified by falling suicide rates around the time of the two world wars.

Financial support and investment in mental health services also help, but there could yet be a later rise if people perceive their post-Covid lives to have less meaning and purpose, or think others are recovering better than they are. More than 1m people in the UK are suffering with long Covid, which can have profound neuro-psychiatric consequences.

The great outdoors

ONE way to reduce fear and anxiety in a pandemic is to emphasise what can be done as well as what can't: "Stay at home or walk outside" would have been a much better message. The chances of catching the virus outside are minimal compared to inside. Most of those infected were sitting or lying still, in still air where the virus hangs around in tiny droplets. So walking in fresh air is a sure way to avoid infection. It also profoundly improves health.

Walking cure

THERE is no drug yet invented which matches the physical and mental health benefits of walking outdoors. It reduces anxiety, lifts mood, helps you sleep better and improves cardio-respiratory, metabolic and musculo-skeletal health. Those who can't walk (or wheel), or who suffer post-exertional malaise when they overdo it, have a good excuse. For the vast majority, the amount of physical activity done over a lifetime increases both length and quality of life, and reduces the risk of all manner of disease. The best way to avoid Covid is not to catch the virus. But if you do, the fitter you are, the far more likely you are to recover.

In 2005, researchers studied 1,705 Australian men over 70 and measured how fast each man walked. Five years later, 266 men had died, but no one who could walk faster 1.36 metres per second at the outset (or 5km/h) had died. As the researchers observed: "Faster speeds are protective against mortality because fast walkers can maintain a safe distance from the Grim Reaper." And coronavirus.

The fitter you are at any age, the less you fall. The more you need help getting out of a chair or off the toilet, the easier you are to infect. The bottom line: if you can walk, walk – quick enough to make you pleasantly breathless but not so fast you can't enjoy the surroundings.

Lessons from smallpox

COUNTRIES have been left to go their own way on Covid, but if we want to control pandemics (or global warming) now or in the future, it requires global cooperation. One solution is to prevent infections jumping over from animals in the first place, which will mean a big rethink in how we treat and eat them. Some outbreaks on a crowded planet will occur by chance, so constant surveillance, preparation, early action and coordinated international responses are needed to prevent outbreaks becoming pandemics.

Ridding the world of naturally occurring smallpox by 1979 required previously unseen cooperation between rival superpowers and impressive execution of eradication plans around the globe. Whatever the motives, it's good to see China helping India with its current Covid calamity, and Norway – having decided not to use the OAZ vaccine for now – lending its 216,000 doses to Sweden and Iceland so they are used before the expiry date.

Money talks

ONE reason the Oxford-AstraZeneca vaccine is declined by some is the rare clotting risk (also shared by the Johnson & Johnson vaccine). Another is the cost. Given a choice, people opt for the expensive vaccine, not the cost-price one. Expect any annual multi-variant Covid boosters to be more expensive. Malaria has killed more people in history than any other illness. It still sickens 200m and kills 400,000 every year, many of them children. The news that the OAZ team may have produced a safe and effective vaccine is welcome, but why has it taken 37 years?

One reason is that the malaria parasite is far more complex than SARS-CoV-2. Another is that it mainly affects poor people in poor countries who can't afford vaccines. Now, thanks to climate change, mosquitoes are moving from equatorial regions to northern latitudes where the rich world resides. Expect more dengue and malaria vaccines soon...

---

13 April: England and Scotland begin vaccinating under-50s. Johnson & Johnson delays rollout of its vaccine in Europe. Sweden now has the most new Covid cases per person in Europe. **14 Apr**: WHO says Covid-19 cases have now risen for seven weeks in a row. **15 Apr**: 77 cases of a variant first identified in India found in UK. Cases in India double in 10 days. **17 Apr**: Global Covid-19 death toll hits 3m, according to Johns Hopkins University. **19 Apr**: PM cancels planned trip to India. **20 Apr**: Despite "possible link" between Johnson & Johnson vaccine and rare blood clots, EMA says benefits outweigh risks. **23 Apr**: India added to England's travel "red list". **24 Apr**: Half UK population has now had at least one dose of Covid-19 vaccine. **25 Apr**: UK to send 600 pieces of medical equipment, including ventilators, to India. **26 Apr**: EU launches legal action against AstraZeneca over its delivery of vaccines.

MD on Keeping up the momentum

Private Eye 1547   Press day: 10 May

2,297 daily cases   **10** daily deaths   **127,609** UK deaths to date

Vaccine bounce

AS MD predicted in November 2020 (*Eye* 1535), a successful vaccination programme has done wonders for Boris Johnson's career, as well as shoring up support for Nicola Sturgeon in Scotland and Mark Drakeford in Wales. Being highly visible leaders during a torturously difficult pandemic has also helped their parties. Johnson will soon give people "permission to hug outside their bubble" using "common sense". Whether this is sufficient to save the union, however, remains to be seen.

Good news on deaths

OUT of 1,000 people in the UK, 998 have not died from Covid. Since 31 January, there has been a steady fall in deaths from all causes, and from 14 March and every week since, our highly vaccinated nation is showing far fewer deaths for the time of year, compared to the average of the previous five years. Given that as recently as 10 January all-cause mortality was 45 percent above average, largely due to 1,300 Covid deaths a day, that is quite an achievement. Scotland hasn't had a single Covid death for nine days. Not only do lockdown and vaccination work to reduce Covid deaths, but also the vast majority of British people consent to them.

Of the two, vaccination has far fewer side effects than lockdown. As of 5 May, 50,682,567 doses of Covid-19 vaccine had been administered in the UK. If the vaccines were causing significant numbers of deaths, as some anti-vaxxers claim on Facebook, this would have shown up in the comparative deaths. The fact that excess deaths from all causes are now much lower than average post-vaccination strongly suggests the vaccines are both very effective and very safe. However, the UK is right not to offer the Oxford-AstraZeneca jab to the under-40s where the risk of clotting is comparatively higher, though still very small. There have been 242 clotting cases and 49 deaths, with 28.5m doses of the vaccine administered.

Lockdowns stop working when you lift them but vaccines protect the individual and the herd, both now and in the future when viral risks are higher (indoors, in winter). The UK, and vaccine manufacturers, are hoping multi-variant boosters for the over-50s will keep Covid in check whatever happens in, say, Asia or South America. But it's equally important to look beyond our borders and help increase global vaccine production and delivery to allow those at highest risk to be protected. We now have a tale of two pandemics, in the rich and poor worlds. And we also need to learn the lessons from Chile...

Chile sources

CHILE secured rapid vaccine deals to fully inoculate its 19m citizens twice over and was only just behind the UK in its speed of rollout thanks to a well-developed public health system, with clinics in even some of the remotest areas, and a national immunisation programme that distributes flu and childhood vaccines every year. However, despite vaccinating more than 7.5m citizens once, and 5m twice, it has experienced a surge in Covid greater than its previous pre-vaccination peak and much of the country was plunged back into lockdown. Why?

The combination of lockdown fatigue, vaccine over-optimism and needing to work led to a fast relaxation in distancing measures. Indoor socialising and overseas holidays were common over the summer, with few border controls and multiple imported variants. At least 70 percent of a country's population needs to be fully vaccinated to have a shot of herd immunity, and possibly 90 percent. Only 26 percent had received both doses when infections surged, and 87 percent of the vaccines used thus far have been the Chinese-made CoronaVac, which appears less effective after a single dose.

The bottom line is that if you ease restrictions too quickly after vaccination, you can still get large outbreaks. The good news is that within those outbreaks, thanks to vaccination, fewer people are dying than previously.

Door to door

SOME ethnic groups in the UK have lower vaccine uptake than others, but this is as much about getting access to the vaccines as vaccine hesitancy. In most polls, fewer than 10 percent of adults in all age groups and across all ethnic groups do not want a vaccine. Pilots are now under way to offer home vaccinations to those at highest risk who have trouble getting to a vaccine centre. Many GPs have done this already.

Ahead of the curve

ONE of the challenges of being ahead of the curve on vaccine roll-out is that you become the test bed for what to do next. The risk of further SARS-CoV-2 outbreaks and variants has not vanished, but the longer vaccines and boosters continue to work, the more freedoms we can enjoy. Much is still unpredictable, but you can't live a life in fear of what we can't yet know.

The government is right to open up gradually, given infection rates are still very high across the world; but it is wrong to promise its roadmap out is "irreversible". With luck, it might be. But if this rapidly mutating virus has taught us anything, it is that you need a safety net for surges. It's fine to hope for the best, but we still need a plan for the worst.

Testing the water

THE UK is testing the water with indoor music events and snooker tournaments, and outdoor sporting events. Condom sales are on the up. Mandatory isolation may be replaced by a daily negative rapid test. All this is experimental, and needs to be properly evaluated.

MD's confidence has also been sorely tested. I was confident there would be no pandemic in January 2020, because we would defeat the

"At last, it finally feels like we're getting back to normal"

coronavirus in the same way we defeated its 2002 cousin. And I was so confident that my home rugby team (Bath) would make it to this year's European Challenge Cup final that I snapped up two of the strictly limited 10,000 Covid experiment tickets for Twickenham on 21 May. I am now faced with the life-changing dilemma of having to support either Leicester Tigers, our biggest rivals, or a Montpellier side full of South Africans. But I have had two vaccine doses, will follow the rules and am confident I won't return home with Covid.

The wonder of science

ONE lesson from Covid is that health on a crowded planet is both individual and collective. The fitter and more mobile you are, the less likely you are to die from Covid (and most other causes). The sicker you are, the more you rely on others to keep you safe. But humans also have the trump card of science.

It is extraordinary what hi-tech medicine can achieve, from saving babies to curing cancer. But it comes at a cost. The bottom line from most of the columns I've written over 30 years is that despite the theoretical wonder of universal healthcare provided by the NHS, we have never invested in sufficient capacity, technology or staff to provide the highest-quality care to all citizens. No other country does either (India only puts 1 percent of GDP into healthcare, with results the world is now witnessing). But the UK – one of the world's richest nations – handicapped the ability of the NHS, social care and public health services to cope safely with Covid by ten years of austerity.

We have now thrown billions at trying to conquer a single virus. Hopefully, we will now see the value of properly funding health and social care for all diseases and for all people. Even if we do, the pandemic has taught us prevention is far better than cure. And no matter how much we spend on healthcare, it will never be able to cope with the demands of an obese, unfit, prematurely diseased nation.

Unsavoury SAGE

"INDEPENDENT SAGE", a group of scientists who set themselves up to provide more accessible and authoritative advice than SAGE itself, recently celebrated the anniversary of their first public meeting. They have doubtless improved transparency by pressuring the government to reveal who sits on the SAGE committee and all the minutes of their meetings, to get a better understanding of "the science" the government claimed to be following. They also released a rude video (now deleted) attacking England's chief medical officer Chris Whitty and the UK's chief scientific adviser Patrick Vallance.

This reveals more about the egos, politics and academic ambitions of the members of Independent SAGE than it does about the CMO and CSA. At its best, science provides a safe context to form a hypothesis, prove it wrong, go back to square one and keep repeating until, say, you come up with a Covid vaccine. At its worst, vainglorious academics rip each other to shreds on Twitter with a certainty that belies the fact that science is built on error and uncertainty.

Scientific split

SCIENTISTS are still split over whether to use our good fortune with vaccines to pursue a Covid elimination strategy (as in New Zealand and Australia), or whether infection is now so widespread globally, and we are such a crowded, busy, connected country, the best we can do is to keep deaths and harm at an "acceptable" level with vaccines as we do with influenza.

On the downside, the SARS-CoV-2 virus is much more harmful than most seasonal influenza viruses. On the upside, the vaccines against it appear to be far more effective. So, with annual boosters, we may keep annual Covid deaths in the flu range.

The honest answer is we can't know which strategy will turn out to

Agitating a vaccine sample

*"You're working, but you're not being
given to the poorest nations"*

do the least harm overall. Boris Johnson's real or imagined comments about "bodies piling high" makes it harder for him to have an honest conversation with the public about what level of deaths is acceptable or unavoidable. And he has made himself a hostage to fortune (again) by ruling out further lockdowns anyway. Professor Neil Ferguson, who initially modelled more than half a million Covid deaths with no lockdowns, is now optimistic no more lockdowns will be needed unless a variant takes off.

Simon says goodbye

SIMON STEVENS has bowed out as head of NHS England at the right time. The vaccine roll-out could hardly have gone better and the NHS didn't crumble in the heat of battle, despite a decade of flatline funding, record waiting times and record staff vacancies.

However, Stevens knows the reason it didn't crumble is the extraordinary dedication of its staff to keep going even in the most extreme situations. Many are suffering trauma and burnout, and yet have a huge backlog of unmet need to try to address, and patients demanding to be treated "now the pandemic is over". More than 400,000 people have been waiting more than a year for an operation, and many are in pain. GPs are fielding thousands of extra calls and delivering record numbers of appointments, yet are still slated in the press for being hard to reach.

Social care is an underfunded disaster the government has sat on for more than a decade, and that too increases pressure on the NHS. Like former health secretary Jeremy Hunt, Stevens had to cope with the twin ties of the destructive Health and Social Care Act 2012 and a decade of austerity. They both left the service having secured a generous funding settlement that may never now be realised. The essential NHS building maintenance backlog alone is £9bn, never mind the fantasy 40 new hospitals Boris Johnson promised when trying to get elected.

Stevens' successor will have a very full in-tray. But at least he will be free to tell all at the pandemic public inquiry, whenever that is. But with the Hartlepool by-election in the bag, local council election gains and his 80-plus Commons majority, Johnson will be in no hurry to have his pre-vaccination record scrutinised.

30 April: Less than 0.1% of people in UK infected with Covid-19, says ONS. **1 May:** Daily cases in India top 400,000. **2 May:** Liverpool hosts music festival for 5,000, to see if mass events cause virus to spread. **4 May:** Government says NHS app update for use as a "Covid passport" will not be complete by 17 May, when international travel resumes. Pfizer predicts £19bn turnover in Covid-19 vaccine sales this year. India passes 20m cases. **5 May:** US supports patent waiver on Covid-19 vaccines. Canada authorises use of Pfizer vaccine on children aged 12-15. **6 May:** England CMO Chris Whitty warns Covid-19 is unlikely ever to be eradicated. Bank of England forecasts UK economy to grow 7.25% in 2021. **7 May:** New travel traffic light system published for England, with 12 countries added to a no-quarantine "green list" from 17 May. Most adults under 40 to be offered alternative to OAZ vaccine. Public Health England declares Indian variant a "variant of concern". **11 May:** ONS analysis of England and Wales care home deaths registered between w/e 20 March 2020 and w/e 2 April 2021 (covering both waves of pandemic) published. It shows:

- Since start of the pandemic, there were 173,974 deaths of care home residents, a 19.5% increase compared with the five-year average (145,560 deaths); of these, 42,341 involved Covid-19 accounting for 24.3% of all deaths of care home residents.

- Deaths of care home residents involving Covid-19 rose sharply in wave one, but there were a higher proportion of deaths involving Covid-19 in wave two (25.7%) than wave one (23.1%). The higher proportion of wave two deaths involving Covid-19 could be attributed to undiagnosed cases in the first wave.

- There were more total deaths of care home residents above the five-year average in wave one (27,079 excess deaths) than in wave two (1,335 excess deaths).

- During the first and second wave, Covid-19 was the leading cause of death in male care home residents, while dementia and Alzheimer's disease was the leading cause of death in female care home residents.

- Dementia and Alzheimer's disease was the most common pre-existing condition found among deaths due to Covid-19 in both male and female care home residents in waves one and two.

"Grandma! I'm finally allowed to see you again!"

MD on An avoidable tragedy

Private Eye **1548**   **Press day: 24 May**

3,022 daily cases   **8** daily deaths   **127,724 UK** deaths to date

The preventable disaster

IT's official: the SARS-CoV-2 pandemic was "a preventable global disaster", according to the final report of the Independent Panel for Pandemic Preparedness and Response (IPPPR).

Over one year, it has conducted in-depth literature reviews and original research, hearing evidence from hundreds of experts and frontline workers around the world and with an "open door" to inquiry submissions.

Its report, *Make This the Last Pandemic*, found that there were, and still are, "weak links at every point in the chain of preparedness and response. Preparation was inconsistent and underfunded. The alert system was too slow – and too meek. The World Health Organization was under-powered. The response has exacerbated inequalities. Global political leadership was absent."

Delays cost lives

THE IPPPR acknowledged how hard people at all levels in all countries worked to tackle the virus, and the speed at which tests, vaccines and drug trials were delivered thanks to open scientific collaboration. But governments did not openly collaborate, nor react with sufficient urgency to the WHO declaration of a public health emergency on 30 January last year. The "golden months" of February and March 2020, when swift action could have saved many lives, were lost.

Those countries that succeeded in suppression took early, pre-emptive action. Those that lost control (often repeatedly) adopted a wait-and-see approach. Wealth was no guarantee of competence (indeed, the wealthiest countries were often the most complacent). However, within and across nations, the poorest and most vulnerable people have suffered more, both from Covid and its socio-economic fallout. The report urgently calls for the fair distribution of vaccines.

Here to stay

THE SARS-CoV-2 virus is here to stay. There is nothing surprising about a new variant (B.1.617.2, first observed in India) spreading more quickly than the current dominant UK variant (B117, first observed in Kent). That's what evolution does to viruses: they get fitter and fitter. There is currently a variant of B117 that may be vaccine-resistant in time. Booster jabs may be needed.

B.1.617.2 has been with us since February, but we imported it in larger numbers in April, allowing it to seed widely around the UK. The good news is that it (currently) appears susceptible to vaccines, so rising infections should not translate into hospitalisations, deaths and long Covid for those protected. However, only a third of people in the UK have had both doses of vaccines. Surge vaccination in the most affected areas will reduce risks, but protection isn't instant. The government decided not to delay allowing indoor gatherings in homes, pubs and restaurants from 17 May. Time will tell if that was sensible.

Act on surges

IF YOU wait to identify a variant of concern in a pandemic, you're too late. This was the clear lesson of the winter, when SAGE urged the government to lock down amid rising infections, but the government delayed acting until the B117 variant was officially identified as the cause. This led to an exodus from the South-east before Christmas, which spread the variant all over the UK and brought more than double the deaths of the first wave.

The government has just repeated the error by waiting until B.1.617.2 was identified as a variant of concern in India before putting India on the travel red list. Infection rates are under-reported in poorer nations, but even based on reported rates it was clear in early April India was at the centre of a rapid outbreak, with higher levels than nieghbouring Pakistan and Bangladesh. This was highly likely to be due to (then unidentified) variants.

From a pandemic control perspective, it made no sense putting Pakistan and Bangladesh on the UK red list on 2 April, but not India. Up to 20,000 people arrived in the UK from India between then and 23 April, when India was added. They were left to their own devices as to quarantine (which isn't very effective). A further computer glitch in test and trace meant many contacts of people carrying the variant were not traced. A lot now rides on how much protection our partial vaccination offers.

Border confusion

PANDEMICS are best managed by swift global cooperation. In January 2020, neither the WHO nor SAGE were recommending border controls or closures on the grounds that they cause economic harm and merely delay spread, unless you keep your borders tightly controlled from all destinations until the whole world is vaccinated.

The International Health Regulations 2005, which govern emergency pandemic responses, declare the need for a balance between the conflicting aims to "prevent, protect against, control and provide a public health response to the international spread of disease", and avoidance of "unnecessary interference with international traffic and trade". Countries that imposed early, unilateral border controls gained better pandemic control with less economic damage. But had the outbreak proved less serious, they might now be facing legal action for loss of trade and restriction of free movement. Give the Brexit context last year, Boris Johnson was unlikely to advocate border controls before the virus had arrived. "Wait and see" became the UK mindset.

Now, 15 months on from the start of the pandemic, Europe still has no coherent border control policy. The EU has delayed its announcement for a fortnight, Spain is welcoming anyone from the UK without the need for a PCR test, Germany is blocking UK traffic because of the B.1.617.2 variant, and the UK is permitting travel to both countries but advising people only to go if it's urgent.

How SARS started in the UK

THE UK's "wait and see" policy proved our undoing. Research by the Covid-19 Genomics UK consortium (Cog-UK) published last June showed that at least 1,356 people had brought the virus into the UK in February and March, leading to a massive first wave. Less than 0.1 percent of those cases came from China. Rather, the UK epidemic was largely initiated by travel from Italy in late February 2020, Spain in early to mid-March, and then France in mid- to late March. Eighty percent of initial cases arrived in the country between 28 February and 29 March.

Had we embraced strict border controls early, or had an effective test, trace isolate system – or preferably both – we might have controlled the outbreak without lockdowns. But the scientific advice to the government at the time was that border controls, test, trace and isolate, face masks and lockdowns either lacked evidence or delayed the inevitable, so herd immunity became the government's default policy, until it realised how many deaths would result and dithered into a late lockdown.

Public opinion

IN hindsight, with a vaccine less than a year away, the UK might have opted for a "Fortress Australia" approach at the outset, only opening up when all adults had been offered both vaccines. It may not have kept variants out – essential goods have to be traded – but it might have kept the numbers down while allowing more freedom to work, study, spectate and party within our borders. But would people have supported stricter border controls?

In a recent Ipsos-Mori poll of 2,007 adults aged 18-75, 79 percent supported stopping people entering the country from countries with higher levels of infection; 70 percent supported quarantining in hotels for those returning from all foreign holidays; 67 percent supported stopping people entering from any other country; and 58 percent supported stopping foreign holidays in 2021.

By contrast, the government advocates a weak and inconsistent traffic light system. After a country is put on the red list, a grace period of four to seven days enables people to rush back to the UK, much like jumping the lights on amber-red. Or they can travel via a lower-risk country and avoid restrictions.

Those on the amber list are expected to quarantine at home for ten days, but notwithstanding government threats of a knock on the door from the "holiday police", it's still a much more permissive border policy than, say, Australia or New Zealand. No surprise it permits viral spread.

Where did all the money go?

A REPORT by the National Audit Office on the government's pandemic response estimates its lifetime cost at £372bn: £62bn on the job retention scheme, £38bn on NHS Test and Trace, £27bn on self-employment income support, £26bn to devolved administrations, £23bn on bounce-back loans, £21bn on business rate measures, £18bn on PPE, £18bn on rail and bus measures, £18bn on business grant funding, £14bn on further health services spend, £10bn on universal credit, £10bn on vaccines, £10bn on VAT measures... How much of the colossal spend and death toll could have been avoided if we'd got a grip on the pandemic earlier? Only a public inquiry can say...

Public inquiry delay

THE public inquiry, starting in spring 2022, is unlikely to report before the next election. Any claims made by Boris Johnson's former brain, Dominic Cummings, can be conveniently referred on. Modelling expert Professor Neil Ferguson told the science and technology committee on 10 June last year that the 40,000 deaths in the first wave would have been 50 percent lower if lockdown had been introduced a week earlier. Why wasn't it? We'll find out in 2027. Or thereabouts.

Putting a figure on it

NOTHING the public inquiry eventually unearths is likely to be surprising. Many countries fell into the "wait and see" trap. Germany and France had similar second wave excess deaths to the UK. The challenge will be for the inquiry statisticians to enumerate how many lives were saved by our pandemic management, and at what cost. And how many more lives might have been saved – and harms avoided – with more competent management.

It should commemorate those lost and celebrate what we did well, particularly scientific collaboration and investment leading to rapid drug trials, vaccine development and roll-out, and the considerable compassion, support and gratitude shown during the pandemic, particularly to key workers (now sadly waning, not least for overworked GPs).

Global reform

THE IPPPR report, meanwhile, argues that the WHO should be strengthened immediately with an increased budget and remit and "a new global system for surveillance, based on full transparency by all parties, using state-of-the-art digital tools". Will China, Russia, the US, the EU and the UK – not to mention assorted dictators around the world – buy into such a spirit of global cooperation? We shall see...

Covid's global consequences

- 148m people infected and more than 3m Covid deaths in 223 countries and dependencies (to late April)
- During the first wave, 228,000 children and 11,000 mothers across South Asia died due to disruptions in health services
- 17,000 health workers died from Covid in the first year
- Lost global output of $22tn in 2020–25
- 90 percent of children missed school
- Substantial rise in domestic violence and early marriage
- 115m–125m people pushed into extreme poverty
- Levels of mental illness rising sharply
- Health and care staff with high levels of distress and burn-out
- In the poorest countries, fewer than 1 percent of people have had a single dose of vaccine.

A PS from 'MD'

EACH country has been unique in its (mis)handling of the pandemic. June 2021 was meant to be a month of celebration for Boris Johnson and the UK, with the fifth anniversary of the vote to leave the EU and the lifting of all pandemic restrictions on 21 June. Alas, "freedom day" had to be put back by four weeks because we let in the Delta variant in large numbers and then allowed it to spread exponentially. The very experienced chief executive of NHS England, Simon Stevens, retired; and Dido Harding (of all people) applied for his job. Johnson then had to appoint a new health secretary after Matt Hancock finally pressed the self-destruct button.

How very British that Hancock's tenure as health secretary came to an end not because of the UK's high rates of Covid deaths and long Covid in the under 65s; or because of the failure to protect care home residents and healthcare staff from Covid. Nor was his departure due to the expensive failings of test and trace, the secretive awarding of lucrative jobs and contracts using personal contacts and private email accounts, or to a failure to declare clear conflicts of interest. The appointment of Gina Colandangelo as non-executive director at the health department (her job being to independently scrutinise the department's work at taxpayer's expense) elicited no sanction – even though she is a very old friend of Hancock's, and her brother is director of a private healthcare firm with several NHS contracts. When Hancock and Colandangelo became a couple, they kept it quiet. It was only when the pair breached social distancing rules under a spy camera that Hancock's game was up.

How dysfunctional can a government department be when the health secretary is secretly filmed in his own office? And when the health secretary himself is secretly using a private but hackable gmail address to conduct government business? It's as if the Nolan principles on ethics in public life never happened.

New health secretary Sajid Javid will doubtless be sweeping the building for bugs. The Good Law Project is gamely trying to get to the bottom of Hancock's Covid contracts, and he has already been in breach of the law once by failing to hand over details. Gaining access to his private email account to uncover the extent of his governmental wheeling and dealing will be an equally lengthy legal affair. By the time the public inquiry kicks in, the account may have long vanished.

No one knows what will happen in the future. But we do know the virus is likely here to stay; and that whatever strategy we adopt, there is no guarantee of success. With evolving variants, herd immunity may never be fully achieved, even with global vaccination. But it still remains our best shot at minimising the harm of the virus without destroying people's livelihoods. Annual boosters are likely to be needed.

A public inquiry may eventually determine how many deaths and how much wider harm, not to mention how many billions of pounds spent on mitigation, could have been avoided had the UK got a grip on the coronavirus pandemic earlier.

Could we have avoided lockdowns altogether with better border control and earlier testing?

Could we have halved our death rates with earlier lockdowns, which were then shorter and less harmful in other ways?

Would our test, trace and isolate system have worked better if it had been built around the expertise of local authority public health teams, rather than outsourced to non-experts?

Could we have kept up "Fortress UK" until vaccinations rode to the rescue? Who knows: we were never offered the choice.

Given the scale of the loss of life, the public inquiry will also have to provide an outlet for the deep grief and anger of the bereaved. There is no doubt both Johnson and Hancock have spouted a lot of nonsense over many months. Indeed, many ministers and advisers have also persisted with a party line they know to be, well, balls. Anyone who says any of the following is either lying or woefully misinformed:

1 We were well prepared for the pandemic
2 Herd immunity was never the plan
3 We put a protective ring around care homes
4 There were no PPE shortages
5 We protected the NHS
6 Our test-trace-isolate system is world class
7 Our border controls are world class
8 Our roadmap out of the pandemic is irreversible

If our political leaders and their advisers really want to be trusted, they need to admit error along the way and learn from it in real time, rather than have it dragged out of them under cross examination at a public inquiry at some point in the future. As Anonymous once put it: "Science. If you don't make mistakes, you're doing it wrong. If you don't correct those mistakes, you're doing it really wrong. If you can't accept that you're mistaken, you're not doing it at all."

"Following the science", a refrain we all know so well now, inevitably involves making mistakes. But if you won't admit them or learn from them, you are, alas, sure to repeat them.

Timeline of the outbreak...

WHILE countries that had experienced the horror of a SARS coronavirus in 2003 were aggressively trying to limit spread of the virus with border controls, test and trace and face masks, such options weren't initially offered in the UK because the experts advising government did not believe they would work. This was based on previous modelling for an infuenza pandemic.

2011 UK Flu Plan: "It will not be possible to halt the spread of a new pandemic influenza virus, and it would be a waste of public health resources and capacity to attempt to do so."

2014 UK Flu Plan: "International travel restrictions are highly unlikely to interrupt the spread of an epidemic significantly."

2016 Exercise Cygnus Modelled for a "swan flu pandemic", this concluded: "The UK's preparedness and response, in terms of its plans, policies and capability, is currently not sufficient to cope with the extreme demands of a severe pandemic that will have a nationwide impact across all sectors." The UK had four years to improve its preparation, but the Conservative government was in the middle of an austerity programme (before miraculously committing £372bn to the pandemic consequences). The UK's stockpile of essential PPE was inadequate and in some cases out of date; and there was no plan for mass testing. With our overloaded health services and shocking levels of obesity and chronic disease, we were sitting ducks.

2017 UK National Risk Register This estimated that 20,000 to 750,000 people could die in the event of a pandemic flu-like illness. However, for emerging infectious diseases (like SARS-CoV-2, for example) it estimated only several thousand people experiencing symptoms, and only 100 fatalities. This was presumably based on Exercise Alice, which modelled a coronavirus outbreak in the UK in 2016 but is currently being kept secret by the government. We need to see it.

October/November 2019 The SARS-CoV-2 virus *probably* arises from a coronavirus that infects wild bats and spread to humans *probably* via an intermediary wildlife host (yet to be confirmed). The precise origin or specific lineage of bats is unknown. It may have originated outside China but the first big outbreak is detected in Wuhan, Hubei province. It may theoretically have emerged from a laboratory; but as the Chinese government is unlikely to hold a public inquiry, we may never know the true origin. The date of the first known human case in Wuhan is a toss-up between 17 November and 1 December.

10 Dec Three people with what became known as Covid hospitalised in Wuhan.

15 Dec Six cases confirmed, most linked to Huanan Seafood Wholesale Market, Wuhan.

23/24 Dec Bronchoalveolar lavage fluid from lungs of patient with unresolving pneumonia at Wuhan General Hospital sent for genetic sequencing.

26/27 Dec More cases of atypical pneumonia with abnormal CT lung scans at Hubei Provincial Hospital. Wuhan General Hospital patient confirmed to have "new kind of coronavirus similar to bat SARS coronavirus".

30 Dec First international alert of Wuhan outbreak, via disease tracking website FluTrackers, and then the Program for Monitoring Emerging Diseases (ProMED) reporting system, run by International Society for Infectious Diseases (ISID).

31 Dec Wuhan Municipal Health Commission advises those with persistent fever and pneumonia symptoms to seek hospital care; public told to wear face masks and avoid enclosed public places and crowded areas. Total cases: 27; serious cases: 7; recovering: 2. No fatalities reported; no healthcare-workers infected; no signs of human-to-human transmission; cause of pneumonia infection still under investigation.

1-3 January 2020 China's National Health Commission orders institutions not to publish information relating to the disease. Li Wenliang, a Wuhan ophthalmologist who raised concerns about the outbreak in late December, summoned to the Wuhan Public Security Bureau and ordered to sign a confession and letter promising to cease spreading "false rumours" regarding coronavirus. He is reprimanded for "making false comments by

announcing the confirmation of 7 cases of SARS at the Huanan
Seafood Wholesale Market" that had "severely disturbed the
social order". The letter states: "We solemnly warn you: If you
keep being stubborn, with such impertinence, and continue
this illegal activity, you will be brought to justice – is that
understood?" Li signs the confession writing: "Yes, I understand."
He dies in February from Covid.

4 Jan WHO tweets: "#China has reported to WHO a cluster of
#pneumonia cases – with no deaths – in Wuhan, Hubei Province.
Investigations are underway to identify the cause of this illness." It
adds: "We do not recommend any specific measures for travellers.
In case of symptoms suggestive of respiratory illness either during
or after travel, travellers are encouraged to seek medical attention
and share travel history with their healthcare provider. We advise
against the application of any travel or trade restrictions on China
based on the current information available."

12 Jan China publicly shares entire genetic sequence of new type of
coronavirus. Work to develop tests and vaccines starts. WHO
travel advice remains unchanged.

13 Jan Officials confirm Covid-19 in Thailand, first recorded
case outside China.

14 Jan WHO says there may have been limited human-to-human
transmission of coronavirus in the 41 confirmed cases, mainly
within families, and risk of a possible wider outbreak remains.
Risk remains "moderate". Reporters from Hong Kong are taken to
a police station after trying to film inside Wuhan hospital.

(Recordings later obtained by the Press Association show Dr
Michael Ryan, executive director of WHO's health emergencies
programme, extremely concerned that China was withholding
information that could help prevent global spread. Heated debate
within WHO about when or whether to escalate risk.)

15 Jan Japan reports first case. Public Health England says no need
to change travel plans to Wuhan as "the risk is low". The WHO
again argues against travel or trade restrictions with China.

16 Jan German Center for Infection Research in Berlin develops
new test to detect novel Chinese coronavirus. Prof Devi
Sridhar, chair of global public health at Edinburgh University

Medical School, tweets: "Been asked by journalists how serious #WuhanPneumonia outbreak is. My answer: take it seriously bc of cross-border spread (planes means bugs travel far & fast), likely human-to-human transmission & previous outbreaks have taught over-responding is better than delaying action."

18 Jan Imperial College London modelling finds outbreak greater than official figures in China suggest. Disease outbreak scientist Prof Neil Ferguson says it is "too early to be alarmist" but he is "substantially more concerned" than a week ago.

20 Jan WHO confirms cases in Japan, South Korea and Thailand.

21 Jan UK's New and Emerging Respiratory Virus Threats Advisory Group (NERVTAG) estimates that closing border to 50% of passengers – their toughest sanction – should not be recommended as it would "only delay an epidemic in the UK, not prevent one". UK keeps its borders open and imports the virus on at least 1,536 occasions from Spain, Italy and France, mainly from mid-February to end-March 2020.

22 Jan UK's Scientific Advisory Group for Emergencies (SAGE) agrees border screening would be ineffective. It recommends leaflets and posters to urge sick passengers to come forward. PHE moves risk level from "very low" to "low".

23 Jan WHO director-general Tedros Adhanom Ghebreyesus says travel bans "can cause more harm than good".

Wuhan (pop: 11m-plus) is sealed off. Planes and trains leaving the city are cancelled; buses, subways and ferries suspended. Seventeen deaths are confirmed, with 570 people infected in Taiwan, Japan, Thailand, South Korea and the US. Chinese Railway Administration figures show around 100,000 people left Wuhan before the lockdown deadline. Construction begins in Wuhan for specialist emergency hospital.

UK Foreign Office advises against all but essential travel to Wuhan (which is already closed).

25 Jan UK Foreign Office advises against all travel to Hubei province.

28 Jan China makes face masks mandatory in affected cities. South Korea, Vietnam and Taiwan also opt for face masks. In the UK, NERVTAG advises there is no evidence face masks reduce community transmission and may add to fear and anxiety. Foreign Office advises against all but essential travel to mainland China. SAGE advises: "Early indications imply some asymptomatic transmission is occurring." However, it also advises: "Currently it would not be useful to test asymptomatic individuals, as a negative test result could not be interpreted with certainty." This may explain why UK didn't ramp up testing capacity: it didn't believe it would work.

29 Jan UK's first two known patients test positive for coronavirus after two Chinese nationals from same family staying at a hotel in York fall ill. A plane evacuating Britons from Wuhan arrives at RAF Brize Norton. Passengers go into 14-day quarantine at a specialist hospital on Merseyside. The WHO's Dr Michael Ryan warns: "The whole world needs to be on alert now... and be ready for any cases that come from the epicentre." Sixty-eight cases confirmed outside China, in 15 countries.

30 Jan WHO raises risk of outbreak from "moderate" to Public Health Emergency of International Concern (PHEIC), praises China's response and says: "All countries should be prepared for containment, including active surveillance, early detection, isolation and case management, contact tracing and prevention of onward spread." It believes it is "still possible to interrupt virus spread, provided that countries put in place strong measures to detect disease early, isolate and treat cases, trace contacts, and promote social distancing measures commensurate with the risk". It does not recommend border controls or face masks.

　　　Confirmed cases worldwide: 7,818, mostly in China, with 82 cases reported in 18 other countries.

31 Jan US suspends entry by any foreign national who has travelled to China in past 14 days, excluding immediate family of US citizens or permanent residents. Restricting travel and only testing arrivals from one country two months after the outbreak started was never likely to work in a hyper-connected world. Like the UK, the US pandemic was seeded from many countries.

3 February In the UK, advice from SPI-M-O is (not surprisingly) highly uncertain:

● Cases of novel coronavirus (2019-nCoV) in China are estimated to be at least 10 times higher than those officially confirmed.

● It is unclear whether outbreaks can be contained by isolation and contract tracing. If a high proportion of asymptomatic cases are infectious, containment is unlikely via these policies.

● Population-wide reduction in contact – e.g. by closing all schools – will impact transmission but how effectively is unclear.

● The estimated mortality rate of those in hospital in China with pneumonia is around 13 percent. Limited evidence from China suggests severe cases are more common in older people and those with other health conditions. How the virus affects children, and children's role in transmission, remain unclear.

● Current estimate of incubation period – the delay between an individual becoming infected and developing symptoms – is on average five days (range: 1–11 days), roughly twice that for influenza.

● The long incubation means those who have had contact with infected people would require lengthy isolation; and that border entry screening is unlikely to be effective.

● If transmission is established in the UK, there will be a delay before accurate forecasts are available. Preliminary forecasts and accurate estimates of epidemiological parameters will likely take weeks, not days, following widespread outbreaks in the UK.

4 Feb SAGE again advises UK government to follow pandemic flu assumptions in Covid planning: "It will not be possible to halt the spread of a new pandemic influenza virus and it would be a waste of public health resources and capacity to attempt to do so." Many public health experts outside government call for much stricter measures based on the precautionary principle.

11 Feb SPI-M-O recommends mass gatherings should not be cancelled. Coronavirus disease 2019 is named "Covid-19".

18 Feb SAGE advises: "When there is sustained transmission in the UK, contact tracing will no longer be useful." Which is just as well as the UK only has capacity to trace five cases per week (requiring 800 contacts). At a push it could manage 50 cases a week.

23 Feb In Italy, cases rise to 150. Ten towns and 50,000 people are locked down in Lombardy after clusters emerge in Codogno. Schools are shut and sports and cultural events cancelled.

25 Feb PHE tells care homes it is "very unlikely that people receiving care in a care home or the community will become infected". Staff are told they need not wear masks, because t hey "do not provide protection from respiratory viruses". "Herd immunity" appears in SAGE minutes based on an Imperial College paper, which says measures that are "too effective" merely delay transmission. It postulates allowing the disease to spread, and "fine-tuning" infections until UK reaches herd immunity.

26 Feb SAGE postulates that suppressing Covid-19 as in Hong Kong and China "would result in a large second epidemic once measures were lifted". The "preferred outcome for the NHS" might be to allow some disease to spread while reducing the peak.

SAGE advises government that restricting activity outside the home, other than school and work, would delay the peak of the outbreak by three to five weeks and reduce overall cases by 50 to 60 percent. It reiterates that school closures are unlikely to contain an outbreak but could reduce the peak if enacted early enough.

Other SAGE modelling speculates that 52,480,000 people in the UK could become infected, 1% of whom will die, with at least 15 percent of the workforce simultaneously off sick at the epidemic peaks.

27 Feb CMO Chris Whitty says mass gatherings like sports events and concerts may have to be cancelled, and schools closed for more than two months, if the UK is hit badly.

3 March SAGE writes: "There was agreement that government should advise against greetings such as shaking hands and hugging, given existing evidence about the importance of hand hygiene." PM Johnson tells a press conference broadcast on national TV: "I was at a hospital the other night where I think there were a few coronavirus patients and I shook hands with everybody, you will be pleased to know, and I continue to shake hands." Government launches "contain" phase of its plan, described as "detect early cases, follow up close contacts, and prevent the disease taking hold in this country for as long as is reasonably possible".

4 Mar Adverts promoting face masks as protection from Covid banned in the UK. PHE says masks are ineffective and urges more hand-washing to delay virus spread, a message repeated many times.

Government publishes scientific advice that cancelling

big public events wouldn't contain the outbreak. SAGE advises government that introducing social distancing measures could potentially decrease total deaths by 20 to 25 percent, and greatly reduce peak of infection.

5 Mar SAGE again refers to a herd immunity strategy, allowing healthier people to gradually catch the virus and develop immunity, while "cocooning" the most vulnerable. The UK's "optimal policy" is to avoid strong measures to suppress the virus early on, allowing infections to develop over summer while suppressing the peak to 4,500 deaths/day, and reaching herd immunity by September. Modelling assumes suppression can be sustained for a maximum three to four months, so introducing early "lockdown"-style measures is judged likely to lead to a more deadly resurgence when they are lifted.

6 Mar Care home staff still follow February guidance that "face masks do not provide protection from respiratory viruses such as Covid-19 and do not need to be worn". NERVTAG says much of the UK's limited stockpile of high-grade respirators is being used up complying with mandatory fit-testing rules and "there are concerns that there may not be enough FFP3 stock for use later on when it may be needed". It explains why masks are discouraged for the public, but recommended for trained healthcare staff who know when to change them "when they become soggy".

10 Mar Cheltenham Festival runs to 13 March

11 Mar Liverpool FC play Atletico Madrid at home, bringing 3,000 Spanish fans to the UK.

12 Mar Government announces end to community testing for SARS-CoV-2 infections and new focus on testing people in hospital and protecting health workers as it moves from the "contain" to "delay" phase.

16 Mar The UK strategy of "herd immunity" (aka "mitigation" or "single peak") aims to reach population immunity in one surge before September, with 40m lower risk citizens taking it on the chin while higher risk citizens hide. Alas, a new SAGE model predicts 259,000 deaths would result, with NHS intensive care capacity overwhelmed eight-fold. The UK has clearly been barking up a very dangerous tree…

Pandemic glossary

ANTIGEN Proteins on the surface of viruses and bacteria. The body recognises an antigen as foreign, stimulating an immune response.

COVID-19 Coronavirus disease caused by SARS-CoV-2 virus, identified in 2019.

EXCESS DEATHS Number of extra deaths over a given period higher than would normally be expected.

INCUBATION PERIOD Time between infection and person showing symptoms.

LATERAL FLOW TEST Rapid test containing antibodies that bind to proteins (antigens) on the surface of a virus if it is present in a sample.

PATHOGEN Infectious virus, bacteria or parasite that can cause disease. SARS-CoV-2 is a pathogen.

PCR TEST Polymerase chain reaction testing is a laboratory method to raise the amount of DNA or RNA in a sample. Used to detect RNA in samples to see if they contain SARS-CoV-2 virus.

R NUMBER Reproduction number – the average number of people one infected person will give the virus to.

SARS-CoV-2 Severe acute respiratory syndrome coronavirus 2, the virus that causes Covid-19.

SENSITIVITY How well a test reports a positive result for people who have Covid-19.

SPECIFICITY How well a test reports a negative result for people who do not have Covid-19.

SPIKE PROTEIN Club-shaped feature on the surface of SARS-CoV-2 virus that attaches to human cells to enter and infect them.

VARIANT New version of a virus that has mutated as it replicates.

VIRAL LOAD Amount of virus carried by an infected person.

ZOONOTIC DISEASE Disease (like Covid-19) caused by pathogens that originally spread from animals to humans.

Those abbreviations...

CMO Chief medical officer

CSA Chief scientific adviser

DHSC Department for Health and Social Care

EMA European Medicines Agency

JCB Joint Biosecurity Centre

JCVI Joint Committee on Vaccination and Immunisation

MHRA UK Medicines and Healthcare products Regulatory Agency

NERVTAG New and Emerging Respiratory Virus Threats Advisory Group

NICE National Institute for Health and Care Excellence

NIHP National Institute for Health Protection (replacement for Public Health England comprising Joint Biosecurity Centre and NHS Test and Trace). Now called the UK Health Security Agency (UKHSA).

PHE Public Health England

SAGE Scientific Advisory Group for Emergencies

SPI-B Independent Scientific Pandemic Influenza Group on Behaviours.

SPI-M Scientific Pandemic Influenza Group on Modelling.

SPI-M-O Scientific Pandemic Influenza Group on Modelling, Operational sub-group.

WHO World Health Organization